MAINE WILD

Adventures of Fish & Game Wardens

VOLUME 1

MAINE WILD

Adventures of Fish & Game Wardens

VOLUME 1

Written by **Megan Price**

Illustrated by **Bob Lutz**

Pine Marten Press
Charlotte, VT

Pine Marten Press

First Edition

Copyright © 2014 by Megan Price

Front cover and book design by Carrie Cook.

Printed in the USA

For information and book orders, visit our website:
www.PineMartenPress.com

ISBN: 978-0-9828872-6-4

Library of Congress Control Number: 2013911040

Answers to your most pressing questions:

Did the stories in this book really happen?

Bear cub rescues gone bad? Chasing outlaws barefoot in
your briefs? Posing for photos with the hunters you just
busted? A woman swinging a pickaxe at your head?
Trust me, I'm not smart enough to make this stuff up!

Have some stories been embroidered just a little?

A whole lot less than, "The one that got away!"

What about the characters?

The characters are composites—bits and pieces of many
individuals. But if wardens and other innocent bystanders
say we can use their real names, sometimes we do.

What about the poachers?

We change their names and some of the particulars
so's not to further embarrass their families.
The scofflaws' shenanigans and convictions are real!

Get Ready..... Here it comes....

Big Legalese Disclaimer

Any resemblance to any individual,
living or dead, is one heck of a coincidence.

That's our story and we're sticking to it.

Author's Dedication

This book is dedicated to

Mary Sheldon, Stephen Sheldon
Sara Jane Lynch & Francis P. Lynch
A. Christopher Price & Joyce Ann Price

*Thank you one and all for your love and support
over the years.*

Warden Parker Tripp's Dedication

To my parents, Lawrence and Muriel (McDonald) Tripp,
for providing me with a childhood filled with
invaluable lessons, love and patience.

To my wife and soul mate, Rita (Durrell) Tripp.
Without your encouragement and unfailing support,
I could not have done this job.

And to our son, Brian Tripp, wife Jillian (Johnson)
Tripp, and grandchildren, Addisyn Belle Tripp
and Alden Parker Tripp.

I cherish the memories made with you.

STORIES

Bear With Me 1

Cranky Cub 27

If You Knew Susie 43

Smelt Help 61

Bragging Or Lying 87

Captain Calamity 111

Bay State Brunch 137

Nearly Naked Nab 159

Spy 187

Disguise 205

Fireworks 225

Raccoon Revenge 243

"He's knocked off the branch and paws at the air, headed for the parachute."

BEAR WITH ME

nother Spring,
another black bear cub call.

Friend and fellow warden, Greg Maher—who
worked the Grand Like Stream District—was on
the phone telling me all about it.

A concerned citizen had spotted a youngster
roaming around Dobsie Locks, at the north end
of Pocumcas Lake, as Greg explained it to me.

"I'm not sure what's going on," the fellow said,
"but there's a little black bear cub wandering
the edge of the gravel road all by itself. It didn't
run off as I drove up—in fact, it ran towards my
car! I stopped and waited and watched it for a
time. No other bears came out of the woods. It
appeared to be all alone."

"How long did you watch it?" I asked.

"Oh, a good five minutes or longer," he said. "I
rolled down my window to shoo it away and then
I drove on down to go fishing for the afternoon.

1

But when I came back a few hours later, it was still in the road and came running up towards my car again. I had some of my lunch left, so I threw it out the window. It gobbled those scraps down in two big bites and then looked up at me begging for more, like a starved dog."

"And still no other bears around?" I asked.

"Nope," he said. "I felt bad just leaving it there and driving off. But I know the rules—I'm not supposed to touch them. So, I'm calling you."

"Okay," I told him. "I'll get out there and take a look."

Wardens did our best to scoop cubs up when it was clear that had been orphaned. It meant a trip to Gray Game Farm—now known as the Maine Wildlife Park. And that's where Greg said he was planning to transport this orphan—if he could catch it.

I knew this was more than a one man job and it sounded like my kind of challenge. So when Greg ended his story, I didn't hesitate.

"You want a hand, Greg?" I said. "Maybe Mike Ayer could help too. How about I give Mike a ring?"

Mike worked the Bangor area. He told me it was his day off, but he'd be happy to come over and help. But he did have a question.

2

"Just how are you and Greg planning to catch this cub, Parker?" he asked.

"I'm thinking I can run and grab the cub or chase him up a tree and nab him," I say confidently.

"Oh," Mike says. I can almost see the sly smile on his face through the phone cord. I detect a good deal of skepticism.

"Well, I certainly look forward to seeing that!" Mike chuckles. "You tell Greg I'll be over as soon as I can."

Mike, Greg and I had all became wardens following our military service. Those lessons were put to good use in the Maine woods. When the three of us got together we were soldiers on a mission.

I drove over to Greg's home in Talmadge and Mike showed up a few minutes after me.

We had a couple of challenges here. First, we had to locate the cub. For all we knew it was long gone.

And once we found it—if we found it—we had to capture it without it maiming us or vice versa.

I'm eager to impress Greg and Mike. And the two of them know it. They've seen my gung ho behavior before and are playing me like a seasoned angler fishing sassy Sunfish.

You know the little fish—they're like puppies with fins. They'll bite a bare hook if you let them.

We decide to pile into the front seat of my truck as it has the most elbowroom. I agree to drive. Greg and Mike will keep their heads on swivels and try to spot the cub.

We tease each other speculating how this is going to go, including who is most capable of chasing the cub.

Both Greg and Mike say they don't run like they used to and would likely flunk any Fleet Feet contest.

"Geez, I hate to admit it, but the cigarettes probably knock me outta the running," Greg says with feigned sadness.

"Guys, you know me. I'd be game if it wasn't for my knee," Mike adds, with a wink at Greg.

They both lean forward and look left at the nut behind the wheel and grin. The fact they both cave so fast was a big clue they want me to volunteer to chase after the cub.

Greg turns to Mike and says in a fake Gee Whizz voice, "Mike, Parker was a track star back in high school. Did you know that?"

"Oh yeah," Mike says, pretending I'm not sitting right next to the two of them and hearing every syllable. "I think I've heard a little something about him winning some award for cross country—about 50 times," he snorts.

Greg looks back at Mike and says, "Well, do you think Parker's still got it, Mike? I mean, there's been a lot of water over the dam since Parker's glory days in high school."

I take my eyes off the road and look right.

The two of them have their heads bowed in concern, like they're watching a beloved, but aged, home run hitter walk to the batter's box with the bases loaded in the World Series. Has he still got it?

There's dead silence for a few seconds until Mike adds, "And there's been quite a few slices of banana cream pie over that dam too."

The two of them turn towards me and double over laughing.

My face turns red. I look back at the road, sit up straighter and suck in my gut. I glance down and see my belt buckle. They're right that it's been a few years, but I think I'm fit.

"You two just find the bear and then we'll see if I've still 'got it'," I say. "And remember, if I have to tree it, you two gotta come up fast with the parachute. We may have to shake it out of a tree."

"We'll see just what kind of a bear dog you are today, Parker," Greg laughs.

"Can't wait to hear him on the trail," Mike adds. He throws his head back and lets loose an "Awww ooooh!" hound lilt, and follows that with the sound of a dog panting.

I shake my head and all three of us laugh like crazy.

It's clear why my two pals allowed me to come along. They're having a terrific time teasing me mercilessly.

But while I'm laughing on the outside, I am dead serious about catching this cub.

And it strikes me maybe I should have a back up plan, just in case this baby bruin turns out to have a very protective mama nearby. That could get ugly real fast. I could end up being the one running scared.

The bottom line for me was, if we spotted the cub but I couldn't catch it, I'd feel like a failure.

My reputation and pride were on the line. I was a racehorse champing at the bit on the way to the starting gate.

The three of us quieted down when we approached the turn to Dobsie. We rolled down the truck windows to listen and I slowed the truck to a crawl.

We looked from left to right and back again. Over and over.

But there was no sign of any cub, only a couple of red squirrels scampering over downed trees.

We stopped about a quarter mile from the end of the road, with still no sign of a bear or any anglers either.

Our back up plan was to check fishing licenses in the area to make good use of our time. Plan B was turning into a bust too.

I threw the truck into park and the three of us got out and walked around the campgrounds and shoreline. There was simply no one around. No vehicles, no one fishing and most definitely no sign of a bear cub.

This was turning into a big waste of warden power.

"What do you think, Parker?" Greg said as we finished a loop through the remote site.

"I guess we might as well head back," I shrug. "There's nothing here."

We walk back to the truck in silence, still looking and listening but hearing nothing more than a Canada Jay and some distant crow calls.

I climb behind the wheel and Mike and Greg slide in beside me.

We were a decidedly disheartened bunch. We're like three guys who climb out of bed at 3 a.m. to race to the charter boat, fish hard all day and return to the dock with nothing more than sunburned necks and an empty cooler.

"Maybe we'll see him on the way out," I say, trying to be positive. Mike and Greg nod.

I spin the truck's nose around and we resume our slow patrol. I'm biting my lip and hoping against hope that cub story is true and he shows himself.

We're a little more than half way to the main road when Greg says, "Hey!" and jabs a finger at the windshield.

There's the round rump of a black bear cub —stubby legs ambling aimlessly up the road— about 50 yards ahead.

My mind screams, "YES!! Go time!" and I floor the gas pedal. I'm afraid the bear will dart into the woods before I can get up to it.

I'm a little too hard on the accelerator. The truck lurches forward and Mike and Greg are thrown back in the seat like reluctant astronauts at a moon launch.

The truck's rear tires spin, spitting rocks and sand for 20 feet.

The cub hears the commotion behind him. He turns and looks over his shoulder. He see's my truck roaring up on him and his eyes go white.

I've spooked him. He bounds off the road and into the brush.

I grit my teeth, lock eyes on an alder where the cub entered the woods and steer right for it.

I get within 25 feet of the tree and slam on the brakes, locking them up.

The truck slides sideways. I throw open the driver's door and bail out of the cab, leaving Mike and Greg to get control of the truck before it goes into the ditch or stalls out.

I know if I lose sight of the cub, I'm done.

A black cub in the shadows of the Maine woods among blowdowns and brush? He's got a lot of places to hide.

But I'm in luck—sort of. I've scared him so

much he is leaping over ferns and through the leaves and making a racket.

He's easy to hear and see. But will he be easy to catch?

I take off after him. I'm sprinting through the leaf litter, leaping over rotting logs and ducking beneath limbs.

He's covering four to six feet in a single stride.

It takes me only a few seconds to realize there's no running alongside and grabbing this cub by the scruff of the neck like some six month old, loose jointed puppy. This creature may be young but he can run.

Treeing him is my only hope.

He is leading me towards a ridge. It's all moss and loose shale and scrawny trees.

I bite my lip and dig in harder, trying to close the gap, to scare him up a tree.

There's a tall skinny spruce 60 feet ahead. He leaps at that tree without breaking stride and sticks like glue to the trunk three feet above the ground.

Then he slides over to the backside—the better to eyeball me—and begins climbing for all he's worth, sending a shower of bark raining down.

I throw my arms up like I just scored Gold at the Olympics. I'm running so hard it takes me five big steps just to stop.

I walk up to the base of the tree and watch as the cub climbs higher.

I bend down to catch my breath and look back for signs of Greg and Mike.

I don't want the guys to see me gulping air. I want them to think I do this kind of thing every day just for fun.

As soon as I can speak, I shout, "Over here! He's treed. Bring the 'chute!"

I back away from the trunk about 15 feet while waiting for the posse to arrive. I want the cub to stay in the tree but not be so scared he goes all the way to the top. This tree he's chosen looks mostly dead.

I don't see a lot of hope for me following him up the trunk.

The tree canopy had blocked most of the sunlight from reaching the ground for many years. The lower tree limbs had all died off.

There are no branches within 18 feet of the ground to support my weight. He's either smarter than he looks or he just got lucky.

I try shinnying up the trunk, but its like trying to climb a cedar fence post. My boots just slide off.

I spot a leaner tree hanging over the crown of the tree holding the cub.

And while this second tree doesn't look too healthy either, I believe I can at least pull myself up it, jump over to his tree, maybe snag the cub or knock it out of the tree so Mike and Greg can catch it.

I hear the guys running up behind me. I wave my arms so they can see me easily.

They climb up the ridge and see me grinning —a man with a plan.

Mike shakes his head. "Well, you got him treed, Hound Dog!" Mike says. "That's really good."

Greg walks around and says, "But this cub sure picked an ugly tree to climb," he says. "It doesn't look healthy enough to support a house cat."

"What's it gonna be, Parker? Got a plan?" Mike asks.

"I think I can scoot up this leaner," I say, walking over to the neighboring tree trunk. "Then, I think I can jump over to his tree and we'll see what happens."

Mike and Greg raise their eyebrows and look at

one another but don't say a word as they study the tree tops.

"It's about a 20 foot fall if you miss," Mike points out. "I doubt we'll be able to break your fall enough to keep you from getting hurt with this 'chute."

"I guess I'd better not miss then," I say, smiling.

I start climbing before the cub gets some other idea about escaping me.

Mike shakes out the parachute folds and Greg grabs a corner and I scoot like a hungry monkey scrambling towards a ripe mango. My behind is up in the air and I am on all fours.

The cub sees the 'chute billowing out just above the ground and me coming at him from a neighboring tree and he decides we are all dangerous lunatics.

He pulls himself farther up his scraggly roost.

He's a good 25 feet in the air now and stepping out on branches you wouldn't think would support a raven.

I have my legs wrapped around the leaner tree and get to about eight feet away from him. I stand up on the leaner, grab a live branch above my head to balance myself, take a deep breath and then leap over into his tree.

He doesn't like this move at all. The tree sways and the two of us swing with it. We're about 10 feet apart.

The bear wrinkles his nose and shows me his teeth.

There weren't that many of them, but what he had was impressive—white, long, curved and pointed. They reminded me of a snarling coyote's chompers.

I try talking to him, but—like a lot of Mainers—he doesn't believe me when I tell him I'm from the government and I'm here to help.

He looks around and starts climbing farther up into the canopy.

I have no choice but to try and follow him. But the tree bends like a bow beneath my weight with every move. It's like the tree is trying to shake me off.

The cub really doesn't like me following him. He turns and says, "Woof!" and chatters his teeth like a wind up denture toy.

He's running out of tree to climb. He stands up on a one inch thick branch while reaching up high with his front paws towards a twig that can't possibly support his weight.

Stretched out like this, and just four feet

from my nose, he looks a lot bigger, and more dangerous, than he had at first blush.

I lunge and grab for the cub. He twists his head and dodges and I snap my hand back.

Mike and Greg are trying to give me advice from below. I can't make out their words because the cub has launched into a snarl. I inch closer.

We stare at each other like gunslingers at high noon waiting to see who will make the next move.

I can see the worry in his eyes. I'm hoping he doesn't see the worry in mine.

The cub curls his lips and snaps his jaws at me. I see him rocking on his hind feet. He's preparing to take a swipe at me or lunge.

Even though he's small, if he attacks me, I'm in trouble. If he knocks me off my precarious perch and I fall to the ground, I really could break my neck.

I have to go for it.

"Get ready, Guys," I shout to Mike and Greg. "He's coming down."

I make a tight fist with my right hand, lean forward and swing my right arm as hard and fast as I can at the cub's midsection, sweeping him off his feet.

His face goes from a nasty growl to a wide eyed "Oh No!" instantly.

He's knocked off the branch and paws at the air, headed for the parachute.

Trouble is, I've done such a good job I've bounced myself out of the tree as well.

I lose my footing and fall after him.

I can't tell you what it looked like to Mike and Greg on the ground, but I have to think they were having second thoughts about playing catcher.

I fall about eight feet, until my belt slams into a branch and I am able to stick my left boot into the crotch of a gnarly limb and snag a branch above me with my right hand. I hang there, a terrified Tarzan for a few seconds.

When I look down, I see Greg and Mike bent over, battling a black blur. Their elbows are seesawing back and forth like world class competitors in a two man saw contest.

Now, the thin tree the cub had chosen is my friend.

Once I get beneath the limbs, I wrap my arms and legs around the trunk, turn my boot heels in and slide down the last 18 feet like it's a primitive fireman's pole.

I shake my pant legs free of bark and needles, brush off my shirt and stroll on over to Mike and Greg.

"How's Woofer?" I asked as the two of them grimace trying to get control of him. It looks like they are wrestling an angry alligator.

"Woofer?" Greg echoes looking up at me.

"When we were nose to nose up there in the tree, that's what he said his name was," I grin.

"If you say so," Mike says, shaking his head. "Whoever he is, he's a fighter! How about you grab him and run him back to the truck before he wriggles out of the 'chute? We almost lost him once already."

I take the cub and the 'chute in my arms and start running. Mike and Greg were close on my heels—so much for their claims of a sore knee and stung lungs.

"I'll drive. You handle the cub," Greg suggested as we got close to the cab. I immediately agreed. Once all three of us are inside and headed down the road, I start rooting around for food I can feed the cub.

Wardens are on the road so much they always have a stash of sandwiches or cookies or jerky in various states of edibility. Maybe all stages of decomposition would be more accurate.

If it's not dry as a rock and covered in green, it's edible in a pinch. If it is dry as a rock and green, well, it just may be a mossy rock. Very few wardens can eat those, though on a long night in the woods, some have tried.

I run my hand under the seat and come up with two grimy plastic bags with sandwiches that don't look too far gone. At least not by bear standards.

Bears love garbage. This should be a step up from that, I figure.

With Mike's help, I open up one bag and tear off a hunk while holding the bear steady on my lap. Next, I try slowly peeling back the layers of fabric from the cub's head.

I feel black fur, black fur, black fur, then an ear and then YEOW! he chomps down on my fingers.

My hand shoots out of the parachute like a rattlesnake has nailed me. Mike tries not to smile.

"You want a glove, Parker?" he asks. I get the sense he has dealt with a few more wild animals than me.

"Yeah, that's a good idea," I say, shaking my hand and counting my fingers. "Try the glove box."

Mike pops it open and digs out a leather glove. I use my teeth to help pull it on, pick up the other half of the sandwich and slowly slide my hand back under the parachute for a second try at feeding Woofer.

He bites me again. But the glove lessens the pain.

I now decide the cub has demonstrated excellent jaw strength and there is no need to hand feed him like he's some sort of invalid. I drop the rest of his meal inside the 'chute and retreat. He'll find it eventually and I will get to go home with all my fingers.

A half hour later, Greg pulls into his driveway and looks at me. "Looks like you got yourself a cub there, Parker!" Mike is already saying his goodbyes, eager to get home while there's sunlight left to tackle some chores.

I hadn't thought this far ahead. I just wanted to help catch a cub. I never thought about what we woud do with him next.

The cub is calmer anyhow. He may even be sleeping. At least he's not struggling to get free.

I've got a truck and a bear in a parachute and some very sore fingers. That's it. I realize that back at my home in Woodland, I haven't got a dog pen or even a shed to put the cub in.

Lucky for me, my wife, Rita, loves the Outdoors as much as I do. I figure she will like meeting this little guy.

So, I say to Greg, "Oh. Yeah. Okay then. I'll take him," and I drive off. The cub is tuckered out and he lies there with his eyes half closed and even appears to doze off once or twice.

When I get home, I pick him up, still in the 'chute, open the front door, step inside, peel back the parachute enough so he can wriggle out and set the bear and his loose wrapper down on the floor in front of me.

I figure he will just step out like a dazed puppy and pad around quietly sniffing at the furniture.

Instead, Woofer explodes like 30 pounds of crazy.

The cub starts to run, but can't get more than 15 feet. He's in an alien world. No grass, no trees. His feet are skittering along polished pine board floors and all around him is furniture and paneling and drapes.

Our young Cocker Spaniel, Rinkin, snaps to attention. She was asleep on the couch when I arrived.

Woofer spies the dog as she lifts her head from her blanket.

The bear bounds over to the Spaniel and they touch noses.

I think, "Uh oh! Vet bill!" and fear one or the other will snarl or snap.

Instead, it's like Rinkin just found her long lost brother—the black one with the pointy German Shepherd ears.

The bear and dog instantly connect. I see two stubby tails wagging.

It's like each of them is saying, "Finally, someone to talk to!"

Rita is at the stove preparing dinner. She's heard me come in and is just about to walk over and welcome me home when our domestic bliss further implodes.

It's like I just dropped two furry tornados into our living room.

The blond Cocker and the black bear scramble, clatter, leap, roll, slide and slam up and over the couch and chairs, into walls. Knick knacks rock and magazines scatter in their wake.

The two of them are having the time of their lives.

I am mesmerized by the action. It's hard not to

just smile and laugh. They made me wish I was five years old and could join them.

The bear chases the dog and then the dog chases the bear and they are both so happy— tongues out and eyes wide—it would all be just ducky if only it wasn't our house they were tearing apart.

Which is what Rita is now trying to point out to me.

She steps cautiously into the living room and looks at me as if to say, "Are you out of your mind?" and I instantly realize letting a bear loose in the house is not one of my smarter moves.

We're a young couple starting out. We haven't got much and what we do have is being destroyed by two boisterous beasts.

Rita shouts, "Parker! Do something!"

I run to the refrigerator.

Rita thinks I'm just hungry and eager to fix myself a snack before dinner. I get a look from her that could melt a glacier.

But I have a plan. I'm thinking I can use food to entice Woofer and Rinkin to choose eating over home wrecking.

The dog knows where her meals come from. She breaks from the chase and comes running into the kitchen, her tail still wagging.

I grab a pack of cold cuts, shut the fridge door, tell Rinkin, "Sit!" and give her a bite of bologna.

Woofer hangs back, very suspicious. His head is low, but I see his nose twitch into overdrive.

I'm able to toss a piece of bologna his way. He finds it, gulps it down and takes a few steps forward to beg for more. I alternate between the dog and the bear.

When Woofer gets to within arm's reach and is busy licking his lips swallowing another meat morsel, I duck down and scoop him into my arms.

Once he stops squirming, I introduce him to Rita—but not too close. The cub isn't yet over his "I'll bite anything but pleased to meet you behavior" yet. Even so, Rita is as enchanted by the cub as I am, and manages to pet him.

All animal babies are cute. But there's a reason millions of stuffed Teddy Bears have been sold instead of Arnie the Armadillo.

Woofer settles in fast. He models the dog's behavior and learns to come when called, sit

and even eat without biting the hand that feeds
him within hours.

That evening, Rinkin and Woofer snuggle up
and share a blanket. They're funny looking pals
—a blond dog and a black bear—but obviously
happy.

Only when I have to go to work the next morning
do I realize I have a problem. The bear can't stay
in the house with Rita. She has errands to run
and her own commute to work later in the day.

The cub has to come with me in the truck. I put
the dog's collar and a lead line on him and off
we go. Rinkin stays home.

We get a lot of stares from people as I fill the
truck up with gas and make my rounds. Woofer
appears to enjoy the attention. He stands on the
truck seat with his front paws on the dash and
watches the scenery go by.

When he tires, he snuggles down beside me like
a puppy, curls up and goes to sleep. I reach
over and stroke his thick coarse coat.

I doubt if I reminded him of his mama, but
having someone warm to curl up next to made
him feel safer, I guess.

I had Woofer with me for just a few days. As
cute as he was, I couldn't deny the obvious.

He had the appetite of an insatiable lion, claws that could easily shred our furniture and was growing bigger every day.

Worse, I was becoming attached to him. He was just a fascinating little guy—intelligent, curious, eager to learn and trusting.

It wasn't easy to let him go. But I drove Woofer over to Gray, wished him well and handed him over to the wildlife experts.

Rinkin was bereft for a day or two. Rita—the sensible one—admitted she missed him too.

I visited Woofer a few times over the years and I think he recognized me.

Of course, it might have just been the cooler full of peanut butter and jelly sandwiches I brought with me each time that made it seem that way.

I guess I will never know.

Later, my thinking all bear cubs were as nice as Woofer about got me killed.

That story's next.

"I'm weighing my options, when the cub
makes a daring ricochet maneuver that about
causes me to crash the truck big time."

CRANKY CUB

 year later, I learned
not all bear cubs behave the same.

Phil Dugas, one of the wardens working the
Jackman patrol, called about another case of an
orphaned cub. This one was found wandering
beside some railroad tracks by workers
conducting routine repairs.

It was thin, hungry and liked the smell of the
sandwiches and chips they had brought with
them for lunch. The fellows had been a little
spooked at first, justifiably concerned there was
a mama bear lurking somewhere nearby.

But after a half hour or so, it became clear the
bear was alone and hungry enough to show itself
in hopes they would take pity on it.

They tossed the cub pieces of their sandwiches
and it quickly began following them around,
although from a distance.

After a couple days of this behavior, the fellows

were able to capture it by tossing a net over it while it was eating. They brought the cub to Phil. That meant another cub needed a ride to Gray. Phil knew I had planned to make a loop of the area that day. Long story, not so short, he was calling me to see if I could give the cub a ride.

Of course, when Phil tells me he has this orphan, I'm immediately reminded of my pal, Woofer. Warm and fuzzy memories of him riding shotgun with me out on patrol, racing around the yard like a goofy puppy, falling asleep in my lap or beside Rinkin—it all comes flooding back.

So, giving a cousin of my good buddy, Woofer, a ride? My pleasure. "10 4," I say. "I can come get him. I'll meet you in two hours at the coffee shop on Main Street."

When I pull up in my truck, Phil is waiting for me. He walks up to my door carrying a cardboard box so tall he has to peek around the side.

"I've got the cub with a collar and chain around his neck in here," Phil explains. "Do you want me to load it into your truck for you?"

Well, I didn't have a truck cap on the back and looking at the size of the box, I could see we'd have to cut the top off it to make it fit inside the cab. And even with that alteration, carrying the box in the front seat would make it impossible for me to use the truck's right side mirror. There would barely be elbow room for me. I figured it would be pretty unpleasant for the cub too—dark, limited air circulation, no room to stretch out.

So, I said, "Nah. He shouldn't be any problem. Take him out of the box and you keep it. Just keep the collar and chain on him and put him here in the front seat. He'll be all right."

Phil nodded, put the box on the ground, opened the flaps and removed a familiar sight—another ball of black fur. This cub was maybe 40 pounds, bigger than Woofer was when I got him, but like Woofer, rail thin from having to try and fend for himself.

I lean over from behind the steering wheel to the passenger side and roll the window down part way, then pop the door open. Phil places the collared cub and his chain on the front seat.

The cub blinks and looks around through sleepy eyes. He's like a Newfie puppy waking up from a pleasant afternoon nap.

I slide across the bench seat, roll the driver's window part way, grab my folder full of paperwork to review with Phil, step outside, then shut the driver's door and lock it.

Phil and I walk inside the diner to take care of business. The day was cold with heavy gray skies and rain predicted for later in the day. There was no danger of the animal becoming too hot in the cab. I hoped he would just go back to sleep.

Like most meetings, this one took about twice as long as I thought it would.

Phil and I go through two cups of coffee apiece reviewing cases. A slice of pie might have snuck in there too.

As I say my goodbyes at the diner door, I notice the cub is standing up on the truck seat, his nose poked out the window, clawing at the passenger door glass.

"Looks like my passenger is eager to get going, Phil," I say and trot to the truck. I unlock the driver's side door and sit down behind the wheel. The cub's back stiffens. He turns his head sideways to look at me with his eyes white, his claws still hooked over the window glass.

I ignore the attitude. I figure he will warm up to me fast, just like Woofer did.

"Hey there, little fella. Sorry to be so long," I apologize and put the key in the ignition. The cub drops down onto the seat, wedges his behind between the armrest and the seat back and glares at me.

He reminds me of a sullen teenager who

expected you to pick him up two hours earlier —before you had that flat tire. He doesn't care that you had to change the tire in the pouring rain. It's all about him.

"Hmmmm. I guess I should have brought you a donut or a sandwich or something," I mumble out loud. "Oh well, you'll be at your new home in a few hours. I'm sure they'll feed you. Just hold on."

I fire up the engine, reach for the shifter on the column and when the truck lurches forward, the cub's eyes go wide and he hunches low—like a cat getting ready to hack up a hairball.

I try to reassure him with my voice. "It's okay," I tell him. He doesn't believe me. Maybe he's heard about my driving from the other guys.

The cub chatters his teeth like a snowmobiler who just pulled himself out of the ice after breaking through the lake.

The hair on the back of my neck rises. I recall Woofer doing this when I was about eight feet away from his nose up in the tree at Dobsie Locks. I'm pretty sure this is Bear talk for, "If you can read this, you're too close."

"Listen, Bear, we're stuck in this truck together for the next 150 miles, so just relax," I tell him, while waiting for a car in front of me to turn left.

I hit the gas hard and pull out of the parking lot onto the main road. I'm hoping he will focus on the scenery and ignore me. But within a quarter mile I can tell he's not much of a sightseer.

He's still backed into the corner and now he is rocking back and forth like a wrestler looking for an opening. I turn my head left to check my side view mirror for just an instant. That's the moment he was waiting for.

The cub springs across the seat and latches his jaws over my forearm like a spiked vise. "Yeow!" I shout. I instinctively yank my arm to my chest and the truck swerves towards the ditch.

Either the rocking truck or my yelp scares him. He lets go, spins and retreats to his corner.

I look down and spy two puncture wounds in my shirtsleeve about three inches apart. It's like someone drove two nails into my arm.

I grip the steering wheel harder with my left hand and shake my head in wonder at this ungrateful Ursus Americanus. What is his problem? It's obvious the nice guy approach is not going to work with this cranky cub.

I try a sterner voice. "Stay over there!" I shout and glare back at him.

There's no hint of an apology on his face.

Instead, his eyes narrow like a gunslinger strolling into town readying himself for a high noon shootout with the Sheriff.

I don't speak Bear, but it doesn't take a zookeeper to know he's saying, "Get used to it, Buddy! That's just a little sample of what I got in store for a crazy cubnapper like you!"

I turn my eyes back to Route 15 before he ends up getting us in an accident. Luckily, there's not a lot of traffic. All goes well for about two minutes.

I hear scrambling. He lunges at me again, bites harder, wraps his front paws around my forearm and starts kicking like a cat with his back feet.

His claws rip me like lawn rake tines on soft earth. I throw my arm up and back, batting him against the rear window, trying to shake him loose. The sudden elevator ride surprises him.

He lets go, scuttles to his corner, turns towards me and hunkers down again.

I look down at the top of my sleeve and now there are four holes in it. I'm pretty certain there's a matched set on the bottom, but I don't want to look.

I start doing the math as to how many holes I will end up with at this rate by the time we get to Gray—which is another 145 miles or so.

It's a lot. I have to convince this cub to stop using me as his chew toy.

Out of the corner of my eye I see his head lower again. He is getting all snake eyes at me. It is clear he's not giving up. He's just looking for another opening when he can make more of an impression on me—with his teeth.

I'm riding the tail of a car in front of me and wishing I had a cage in the back of my truck. This bear might be small in size but he is very big in attitude. I'm wondering if maybe there's some brown bear blood in this cub.

I consider radioing Phil to come get his bear or at least bring me that box, but I don't want to admit I'm having trouble handling this cub.

I'm weighing my options, when the cub makes a daring ricochet maneuver that about causes me to crash the truck big time.

He leaps at the dashboard, bounces off it and with jaws and claws ready to rumble, he jumps on my chest. I throw my left arm in front of my face to block him while keeping my right hand on the steering wheel.

The cub bounces off my left forearm, slides off the steering wheel, twists in the air like a tuna, slips over and behind the dash and the wheel and slides to the floor, snarling and spitting all the way.

His chain follows, rattling like rivets popping, behind him. Trouble is the links grab onto the steering wheel knurls, and his chain gets all boogered up.

I weave like a drunk down my lane. It is like he's trying to drive now. I've lost control. I grasp the steering wheel hard with my right hand and attempt to loosen his chain with my left.

It's like trying to untangle fishing line. It's a two hand job and one that should not be done while driving at 50 miles an hour. My left boot goes for the brake.

No dice. There's a bear there and when I try to push him aside with my boot, I find he's managed to wrap the chain around the pedal too. I can feel him frantically rolling, clawing at my legs and biting my heel.

He's chewing on the leather like its beef jerky and he hasn't eaten for a week. It is not terribly painful, but it is definitely annoying and he may cost me a new pair of boots if he keeps gnawing on them.

I don't intend on us dying here together.

I realize I can't get to the brake and the steering wheel isn't cooperating because some chain links are caught up in the steering column.

I take my foot off the gas and try to roll to a stop.

Just when I think it can't get much worse, he moves away from my boots and sinks his fangs into my left calf.

"OW!" I yelp and leap off the truck seat like my commander just walked into the room and I must stand and salute.

My head slams the headliner and I see stars.

This hurts bad. I try to kick him loose. I shake my leg like a very unhappy cat climbing out of an ice cold flea bath.

The cub likes me fighting back. He reaches higher with his claws, rips at my thigh and bites me just below my left knee.

I don't know what we're fighting about, but he is definitely winning.

If he keeps at it, I will lose a leg by the time we get to Gray.

"Ow! Ooo! Geez!" I am wincing with every chomp.

I pull the truck over hard towards the first bit of gravel shoulder I see and yank on the emergency brake. The truck slides to a stop. I throw the transmission into park and open the driver's door.

The cub lets go of my leg and makes a lunge for the Great Outdoors. He hits the ground running but the chain attached to this collar pulls him up short within three strides and he flips onto his back.

He's furious. He claws at his collar with his front paws and kicks at it with his back legs.

I crouch down beside the truck unwinding the chain from my brake pedal and steering column. I'm worried he might slip out of the dog collar and keep looking over my shoulder.

He's heaving every which way on his end like we are in some sort of tug of war. He's sure not helping me help him.

It takes me a minute, but I am able to unwind the chain from the brake pedal and then rip it out of the slot it found in the steering column. I loop the chain neatly and turn to face the troublemaker on the ground.

He feels the tension on his collar change from a dead stop to where it has some give.

He rears up on his hind legs and throws himself forward like a big Belgian pulling horse twitching a massive load at the Bangor State Fair.

I lean back and yank that chain hard. He flips in the air onto his back on the grass and digs at his collar with all four feet, then gives up, gets himself upright and prepares to make another run for it.

I take three big leaps, bend low and grab him by
the scruff of his neck.

He utters a baby bear roar of frustration,
throws himself onto the ground and spins like
an alligator trying to shake me off.

"No way, Buster!" I mutter through clenched teeth.

I lift him off the ground so he can't use his
claws to dig in and take off. He squeals and his
legs spin like eggbeaters as I carry him back to
the truck cab.

All the way there, he tries to turn his head
around and grab my forearm like a snake.

I have to give him points for persistence. This
cub has no interest at all in making friends.

I know I have got to tie his chain into my truck
somehow as far away from me as I can. Maybe I can
run the lead through the passenger door armrest?

I push him through the driver's door and onto
the floorboard as far from me as I can get him
and reach behind the seat for anything that
might help me.

My hand lands on slippery quilted fabric. I pull
hard and out pops my snowmobile suit. It's a
little big for him, but I'm thinking maybe that's
a good thing.

I open up the suit on the passenger side floor, while the bear squirms angrily in my other hand. Then I set him down quickly and wrap him up fast—a frenzied fajita.

I hold him still for a minute, wrapped in my green padded suit like a papoose. There was just the three inches of his snout sticking out so he can breathe.

I don't say a word. But I'm looking around the cab just in case this maneuver doesn't work out.

To my surprise, I feel the cub's body begin to soften. He stops struggling.

Maybe he likes the dark. Maybe he thinks he's in a cave. Maybe being all trussed up makes him feel safer.

More likely, he is just all tuckered out from using me as his chew toy.

I don't know. I just know it works.

I close the passenger door gently and scoot around the grill, slide back into the driver's seat, softly close my door, exhale big and throw the truck into Drive.

I drive the final 100 miles in a bit of a hurry, with my fingers crossed this cub is done attacking me.

I kick myself for being naïve enough to think all black bear cubs would behave like Woofer.

I keep glancing over to the right. I see my snowmobile suit rise and fall with the cub's rhythmic breathing, but he never stirs.

When I pull into the game farm, I breathe a big sigh of relief. I roll to a stop so as not to jolt the cub awake. Then I slide out of the driver's door, run to the passenger door, open it quickly and scoop the cub up, still wrapped up in my snowsuit.

I feel him stir inside his wrap. He's kicking his feet and squirming. It's like wrestling with a coiled spring. This baby bruin wants to brawl.

The wildlife folks had been waiting for me. I run with the squirming cub to a pen they have readied for him. A young woman opens a heavy screen door and I bend and unfurl the cub from my snowmobile suit. He rolls into his new home like he's a frankfurter slipping out of a roll slathered with mustard.

He leaps to his feet, spins towards us, lowers his head and snarls big at me one last time. Maybe that's his way of saying, "Thanks for the ride, Warden," but I doubt it.

I shake my head, turn to the young woman and say, "This cub can be a little cranky. Don't turn your back." She nods and smiles like Mona Lisa as she notices my torn shirt and trousers. She is nice enough not to laugh.

When I arrive home, I find my arms and legs look like someone has dragged me naked through a raspberry patch—several times.

I soak in a hot bath dosed with handfuls of Epsom Salts for 30 minutes, then paint the bigger holes with that orange stuff that stinks and stings.

When I'm done connecting the dots I look in a mirror and realize, "Now, I look like I've been hit by orange buckshot too."

That's the night I decided I would leave the wildlife rescues to others. I'd stick with chasing Maine's two legged animals.

Sure, I might get shot at and there may be brawls and broken noses.

But at least no angry guy would ever try to eat me alive.

"I wasn't fishing," she says,
looking at me like I am crazy.
"I'm pregnant."

IF YOU KNEW SUSIE

I'd purchased a motorcycle that was neither new nor fancy—it didn't have a big engine— but it was nimble, with good clearance. I could maneuver over rocks and downed trees in the forest and it was fast enough so I could ride the main roads too.

The bike allowed me to check anglers on small streams deep in the woods and remote ponds where a lot of people think a warden will never find them.

I wore coveralls over my uniform and a helmet to be inconspicuous. I looked the same as a lot of dirt bike riders. And I was having fun. But tucked in my breast pocket was my citation book and in my pack, lashed to the bike's rear rack, were my binoculars and other gear.

I had already caught one fellow well over the limit on brookies in Waite, earlier in the day.

Now, I was working my way down towards Grand Lake Stream, on my way to Monroe Pond. The two bodies of water are split by a gravel road and share the name.

I parked my motorcycle out of sight and strolled on over to the smaller pond and scouted the perimeter.

Neither pond was stocked at the time. Most anglers fished the bigger one.

I raised my glasses to my eyes and took a slow look around.

Nobody there.

On a hunch, I left my motorcycle, crossed the road and hiked back to an arm of Monroe Pond that not many people frequented. There was a nice little knoll and from it, I could scan the entire perimeter.

I could take my time up there and watch without anyone seeing me.

I didn't really expect to see anyone fishing. It was the middle of summer and a beautiful day, but it was also the middle of the week and most people had to work.

But, off in the distance, I saw a couple—a man and a woman standing maybe 40 feet apart, both of them with fishing poles in their hands.

I stood up, leaned against a big Spruce to steady the binoculars and watched them for a half hour.

They appeared to be in their early 20s, both wearing jeans and rubber boots to keep their feet dry. She had on a blouse that billowed out over her abdomen. The woman was clearly pregnant, with a firm round belly pooching out from beneath the white cotton folds of her shirt.

I see the fellow reel in a fish, check it for length and put it in his creel with a smile on his face and a few words to the woman beside him. She doesn't gush over his catch.

I was a good 100 yards away, but from the size of the fish and the way it behaved as he reeled it in, I was pretty certain he'd caught a brook trout.

I waited another 20 minutes to see if the woman was going to have any luck. She did a lot of casting and reeling in, but patience did not seem to be one of her virtues.

There was something about her stance and the way she was shifting her weight from one foot to the other, and jerking the rod out of the water, that inferred impatience.

For every cast the man made, she made six.

Anyone that knows fishing, knows fishing is a waiting game.

Could be her back was hurting her from

carrying an extra 50 pounds of baby. Could be fishing wasn't her idea of a great time. Could be the bait she was using was wrong. Could be a lot of things. Standing there watching anglers as much as we do, sometimes you want to give people fishing advice so they might be more successful.

After nearly an hour of watching the couple, it is time to hike down along the trail and introduce myself.

I wriggle out of my coveralls, hang them over a broken branch and pick my way along the trail until I am 25 feet away from the young man whom I had seen catch a fish.

I step out of the woods. The woman is nowhere in sight. I figure she has moved down around the bend to try her luck.

I shout out a "Hello! Game Warden!" and smile.

He tells me his name is John and adds, "Uh, I didn't expect to see a warden back here."

When someone says that, it can be loosely translated as, "Oops. I just got caught."

Fact is, you should always expect to see a warden when you are in the woods hunting or fishing. That's our job, right? To be where no one thinks we are.

John looks at me with a crooked smile, shakes his head and sighs.

I get the impression he has heard this kind of logic from her before and had learned to just let it slide on by, like a plate of raw oysters at the bar. You just let 'em slip down your throat and don't bother to chew 'em, because if you do they might very well come back up.

I turn to the wife and point to the far side of the pond.

"I was standing over behind those trees for close to an hour. I saw a fishing rod in your hand and I saw you cast and reel in your line repeatedly," I say, looking her sternly in the eye.

I make a point of speaking clearly and slowly so she will understand me.

She crosses her arms, clenches her teeth and won't answer me.

"I saw your husband catch a fish and put it in his creel and I saw you fishing," I glare at her.

Out of the corner of my eye, I see John is licking his lips. He looks down at the gravel beneath his feet and shakes his head.

His shoulders begin to sway slightly. It's clear he's very uncomfortable with me challenging his wife.

The wife glares back at me, sets her jaw and plants her feet.

"I was not fishing, I'm pregnant," she says again and she looks at me like I am from another planet—a planet populated by uniformed idiots.

I can see getting a straight answer from her is not going to happen anytime soon. I sigh, turn to John and ask, "Does she have a fishing license?"

His head goes lower, his mouth twists into a strange shape like he has gas.

"No," he says sheepishly. "I told her she wouldn't need one. I didn't figure a warden would be checking licenses way back in here." His voice trails off into a faint mutter and then a sad sigh.

He looks up at me and says, "This is my fault."

He's like a Maine camp owner who knows if he had just taken the garbage to the dump on Saturday instead of watching the big game on TV, the bears would not have broken into the cabin and torn the place apart on Sunday while the family was away at church.

"What's your wife's name?" I ask him. I figure she won't give it to me if I ask her directly.

"Susie," he says.

I turn back to the woman and say, "I'm sorry, Susie, but I am going to have to give you a summons for fishing without a license."

Well, you would have thought she was being charged with murder.

Her eyes go from their gritty gunslinger slits to wide open, wild fury. She begins spinning in circles and flailing her arms like a hornet had settled into her hair.

She shouts at the top of her lungs, "I wasn't fishing, I'm pregnant!" and then she calls me names the most seasoned sailor in the grimiest biker bar in Belfast would be ashamed to use in public.

It was some salty spray.

I hoped the baby was covering his ears. I wish I could have.

John and I take two big steps back and we both stare at her—speechless.

Susie is stomping, swinging and swearing like she is at some head pounding, heavy metal concert.

In another circumstance, I would have said something.

But seeing as how Susie is seven or eight

51

months along in her pregnancy, I don't want
to do anything that might trigger an early
delivery.

I decide to just let her dance out her anger.

Problem is, a minute or more into this rant
—when most people would be winding down—
Susie is gaining momentum. She's like a funnel
cloud about to touch down and spin itself into a
tornado.

I watch as she lifts her head and looks towards
the tree line searching for something. She takes
three big strides, reaches over and grabs her
fishing pole from where she had left it, turns to
look at me and screams, "Watch this!" and with
an insane glint in her eyes and a mad cackle,
she throws the rod up into the woods where
it goes sailing end over end, shredding leaves
along the way.

I think, "Not a bad toss. Susie might have a
future in the ax throw."

She spins back to face John and me, laughs like
a madwoman and shouts, "Happy now?" and
turns away to sputter and stomp some more.

I'm not sure if her comment is directed at John,
at me, or both of us.

I'm also wondering how she thinks throwing

her fishing rod into the woods means she wasn't fishing earlier and doesn't have a license.

I turn to John for some sort of explanation. I don't say a word. I guess the stunned look on my face says it all.

He tries to explain his wife's behavior.

"Oh, I am so sorry," he says in a soft voice that reminds me of a too sincere funeral director. "So sorry. Susie is a little emotional these days. She really doesn't mean it..."

Well, I have a job to do regardless of Susie's antics. So, I reach into my breast pocket for my pen and summons book.

John purses his lips and nods with silent acceptance when he sees me preparing to write Susie a summons.

Susie is now 20 feet away, doing her war dance. I ignore her.

I ask John for their home address and Susie's full legal name. John cooperates and without any fuss, quietly answers my questions.

But when Susie looks over her shoulder and sees John assisting me—conspiring with the enemy from her perspective—it is more than she can stand.

She comes stomping back over to the two of us,
slams the brakes on her sneakers 18 inches
from my nose and roars, "I demand my rights!
I want a trial! I want a trial in Wells! I'll take
this all the way to the Supreme Court!"

She's so upset there is practically steam coming
out of her ears.

John looks up from my summons book and asks
with quiet curiosity, "Do they have trials for this
sort of thing?"

Susie stops yelling long enough to listen to my
answer.

"Yes, your wife can have a trial," I tell him. "But
it would be in Calais, not in Wells."

When Susie hears she would have to appear in a
Calais courtroom to contest the charge, she gets
all fired up again.

Her arms reach for the sky like she is a member
of a Pentecostal Church getting a message from
above. She stumbles back three big steps, turns
and screams, "Calais! Calais!" like a parrot
that has just learned a new word and wants the
world to know it.

"Calais! Calais! Calais!" she screeches and runs
in circles, her platinum blonde curls bouncing
like a dandelion gone to seed.

I've seen enough.

I hurriedly finish writing her summons and separate the white copy from the carbon copy. I hold it out for John to take it.

John looks wistfully at Susie running in circles and shouting across the pond. He sighs and says, "This is our last vacation—just the two of us, I mean—before the baby gets here."

I bite my tongue.

Susie sees me handing John her citation. She circles back and runs behind the two of us and makes a grab for John's fishing rod resting on the forked stick.

She spins back around and with an evil glare swings the pole as hard as she can at my head.

John jumps in front of me and she laces her husband a good one over the head with his fishing pole instead of me.

I'm beginning to wonder if maybe Susie was bitten by a rabid animal a few days earlier. Her behavior is beyond bizarre.

She doesn't apologize to her husband for whacking him in the head. Instead, she raises the rod tip for another murderous try at me.

Being whipped with his own fishing rod finally awakens the beast in John.

His eyes narrow, his pigeon chest fluffs up big. His hands fly up and he blocks Susie's swing with his forearm while his other hand grabs her wrist and holds it tight as a vise.

"Enough!" he shouts inches from her nose.

Susie lowers her arm slowly and she drops the rod. She stands quietly for the first time since I began speaking to her.

There's dead silence for a count of five as the two spouses glare at each other. Then John lets Susie's arms go free. She turns and walks away.

John looks at me and his shoulders slump as he returns to his obsequious self.

"I'm so sorry," he says again. "My wife didn't mean to do that."

I'm impressed with the man's composure. He reminds me of a funeral director who desperately wants your business.

"Really, she's a very nice person," he says.
"Of course," I say and nod.

I could charge Susie with attempted assault.

But as she didn't hit me, and I have no interest in taking a pregnant prisoner with a filthy parrot mouth to jail on the back of my dirt bike—or even worse—be forced to spend an hour or two with her here waiting for a state police cruiser to show up and take her to jail, I pass.

My handcuffs stay on my belt.

But I didn't dare take my eyes off her, even for a second. I had a sense sassy Susie wasn't done yet.

And sure enough, while John is busy apologizing to me, he loosens his grip on the rod he had taken from her. The tip leans close to Susie.

She sees her chance, reaches up and grabs again for his fishing pole, yanks on it and adds a blood curdling scream for effect.

Wildlife within a five mile radius bolts.

For John, this is the final straw.

He yanks the pole out of her hand and hides it behind his back.

"Go up to the cabin and stay there, before you end up in jail!" he hisses at her.

And just in case she didn't think he was serious, he screams, "NOW!" so loud his command echoed around the pond.

Susie stamps her foot, spits at the ground, spins away and stomps her way up the trail, snapping boughs as she goes.

The two of us watch in silence as she disappears into the woods.

We both breathe a sigh of relief.

I snap the aluminum cover on my summons book shut, tuck it and my pen in my breast pocket.

John takes a deep breath, smiles wanly and with sweat running down his face, says again, "I am so sorry. Honestly, my wife is a very, very nice person. She just hasn't been herself lately."

I wonder if he just follows Susie around apologizing over and over again for her.

I rack my brain for something appropriate to say. I haven't run into a situation like this before.

Before I can find the right parting words, John looks down at the summons in his hand and then back up into my eyes.

He looks like a dog begging you not to leave it behind.

"You're lucky," he says.

"Why's that?" I ask.

"You get to walk out of here, ride off into the sunset like in the movies, a free man," he says with the emphasis on "free."

His gaze turns up the trail Susie just stomped on the way to their honeymoon cabin.

"I've got to stay here," he continues, "just me and Susie, for another four whole days."

Well, what could I say? I'm a warden, not a marriage counselor.

I can't wait to get out of here. For all I know Susie is in the cabin sharpening a steak knife with my name on it.

So, I just smile and say, "It was nice to meet you, John."

And I meant it. It was nice to meet John—just not Susie.

"Let me see your net.
Maybe there's something
wrong with it."

SMELT HELP

I met all kinds of colorful characters working undercover at smelt runs.

For folks who don't know a smelt from a lemon sole, smelt are sardine sized salmon—their bigger cousins who get all the attention.

Smelt swim up narrow streams in the Spring to spawn. They are finicky fish and their runs—which occur mostly at night—are notoriously erratic.

So, when smelt lovers find a smelt run, they have to act fast.

A smelt angler's gear is pretty simple. You need a current fishing license, warm clothing, rubber boots or waders, a dip net and a bucket. A flashlight to keep you from breaking your neck walking in and out of the woods is another good idea.

The net is the important thing. It has to have tiny holes. Smelt aren't much bigger around than a pencil and only about half as long.

And maybe it was just Spring Fever, but very often we would find smelt anglers with a net in one hand and a beer can in the other and their pail tied to their belt or juggled somehow.

Smelt fishing and beer drinking just seemed to go together for a lot of the people I caught breaking the law.

This is probably because catching smelt is about the easiest fishing there is, once you locate them. If you can bend your knees, dip a net, pull it up and dump it into a bucket, you're good to go.

That's a problem for smelt. Which is why wardens work hard to protect the fishery.

When Greg and I were working our section of eastern Maine, smelt dippers were limited to just two quarts a night.

That's not a lot of fish. A guy with a big appetite could fry up two quarts of smelt and eat them all in one sitting.

So, like every other kind of fishing and hunting, there are always people trying to take more than the law allows.

Smelt anglers had a number of techniques to cheat.

First and foremost, was sneaking in to dip for

smelt on streams where smelt fishing wasn't allowed at all.

To protect the resource, some streams were flat out posted against anyone taking any smelt. But that didn't stop some people.

It wasn't unusual for us to catch men, women and even entire families sneaking onto a posted stream with nets and pails in the middle of the night.

Some people thought they could beat a warden by bringing their dogs with them. I guess they thought the canines would bark if they spotted a warden.

That usually didn't work out well. A lot of dogs crash through the woods, panting and squealing at the smells all around them. Some would bark at a deer or a rabbit. Some would bark at other poachers on the stream.

As often as not, dogs helped lead a warden right to their poacher owner.

Other anglers pulled the trick of finishing a beer and then tossing the container into the woods with flair—waiting for a warden to come out of the woods and write them up for littering.

The theory here was a conviction for littering wouldn't cost them as much money and they wouldn't lose their fishing rights for at least one year.

If they were going to be caught, they'd prefer it to be for littering rather than illegal fishing.

There were times I had to duck my head so's not to get hit in the head with a bottle or a can coming at me in the dark.

Other anglers trying to get a warden to show himself would act like we were playing Hide and Go Seek.

They'd sneak up to a stream to scope it out first. They might just briefly shine a flashlight to see how the fish were running and peer into the brush for any sign of a man or woman with a badge.

They would have left their waders, net and bucket back in their vehicle.

Once these fellows determined the fish were running, some of them would shout out into the night, "Okay, Warden. I know you're out there! You might as well just come on out."

I always wondered what logic these guys used. Did they think a warden was going to stand up and shout back, "Ah, geez. Yer right. You got me!"

If we were kids playing the game, the next step would be, "Okay, now it's your turn to wear the badge and I'll go be the poacher!"

Did they really think that was going to happen?

We'd sit quietly and if they came back and dipped some fish, we had them cold on a posted stream.

Once they were confident the coast was clear, they would race back to their vehicle, pull on some rubber boots, grab their net and bucket and hightail it back to the stream to dip and fill a pail.

Step up and say, "Stop right there! Warden!" and some of them would sigh and say, "Ahhhh! I knew it!"

Often, some degree of inebriation was required to give guys the courage to break the law. They'd come in packs of two or three or more, each with a can or bottle of some alcoholic beverage, to inspect a stream.

Sitting on a hillside watching the antics from a distance on a moonlit night, I was sometimes reminded of geese inspecting a potential nesting site. There would be a lot of neck craning, body swaying and discussion, as the group stared into a stream trying to determine how good the smelt run was and every now and again jerking their heads up to look for a fox... or in this case, a warden.

Once the group convinced themselves they weren't being watched by the law, the business of smelt dipping would get underway in earnest.

The goal was to dip fast and fill as big a pail as they could carry, then run to their vehicle and drive away without getting caught.

One of the tricks anglers used to muffle the sound of dipping was to split a rubber hose in half and either glue or stitch it to the rim of their net.

That would deaden the sound of the net scraping along the gravel bottom of a stream —making it harder for a warden to hear.

Of course, if you are drunk, stumbling up a rocky stream in the dark, loading up pails with smelt and whispering to your buddies, it is kind of naïve to think a piece of rubber is going to save you from a warden. But that didn't stop folks from trying.

Get caught and one of the favorite excuses was they were just out there to get some smelt for dear old granddad, because he just wasn't well enough to get into the woods and dip for smelt fish himself anymore.

That's kind of like saying, "Granddad can't steal candy from the store counter and run like he used to. So, I'm here stealing for him."

That makes a lot of sense, right?

It was also common for guys to about jump out

of their skins when I stepped out of the woods and said, "Warden!"

Their favorite trick was to try and spill the contents out of their pail into the stream when they saw a warden approach.

If all the fish swam away, it would be hard to prove how many they had taken. This trick only worked on open streams where fishing was permitted, of course. On closed waters, all I had to do was prove they were fishing.

But some fellows got so flustered when they saw my badge, they actually caught themselves.

I had one guy who got so shook up, he forgot where he was.

He spun around and tossed the contents of his pail off into the dark—thinking the fish would float downstream and disappear into the night. There would be no evidence to charge him with catching more than the limit on this two quart stream.

He forgot he was two feet from the shore. He turned away from me and threw his entire catch up onto the bank.

I took two big steps and pulled the little fish he'd caught into a pile and slid them into the pail I was carrying—the one with the measuring line for two quarts on it clearly marked.

Voila! He was well over the two quart limit and left the stream with a citation and a very red face.

Still other guys would cheat by dumping fish inside their waders or in plastic bags they had sewn to the inside of their waders.

That has got to be a creepy feeling—ice cold water along with flopping little fish slapping against your body—or worse, dripping down your legs to your ankles as you walk out of the woods.

Do you tell grandma how you stored 'em before she breads them and fries them up and serves them for dinner?

We'd catch most of these guys next to their vehicles. When they took off their waders for the ride home, they often spilled some fish or acted funny. Ask to look at their license, ask to check their pail and then a look at their waders and that game was over too.

Now and again, the alcohol consumption would get a fellow in serious trouble.

I caught one guy who was so drunk fishing posted waters I was concerned he would fall face first into the stream and drown if I left him there alone.

It happened along a closed section of Sparrow Brook in Oxford County. I found him staggering in the stream with just a pail in his hand. He'd lost his net and he was soaking wet from having repeatedly fallen into the stream.

I asked him what was going on and he told me in very slurred speech that his friends were upstream somewhere. He was trying to find them.

I told him to grab onto my belt when I turned around and to walk with me. He nodded to indicate he would try.

I turned, flipped up the back of my jacket and he muckled onto my leather belt.

I decided to lead him up out of the woods to the parking area where I could find his friends or at least their vehicle. I knew a shortcut.

I managed to get him out of the stream by dragging him, but as we attempted to climb the trail, his legs turned to rubber.

It was like towing a car with a broken tie rod—he was weaving all over the road. I was concerned he'd poke his eyes out or slam his head into a tree trunk and knock himself out cold before we got to the main road.

We came upon a 15 foot deep ditch with a log dropped across it for a footbridge. It was why a lot of people took the long way to the stream.

I stopped and showed it to him and said, "You go first and I will hold onto you to steady you from behind."

You would have thought I'd just asked him to walk out onto the window ledge of the 100th floor of a New York City skyscraper.

His eyes got huge, he stumbled back, shook his head from side to side and slurred, "Unh, Unh! I'm not doin' it. I can't."

I had already lost a good 15 minutes of watching other people fish illegally. I wanted to get back to where the action was. I was not happy I had to babysit this guy.

But I couldn't leave him. He might hurt himself badly or wander off and die of hypothermia. It was a cold night and he was sopping wet.

I didn't have time to argue with him.

He was mumbling protestations and weaving from side to side, when I bent low, grabbed him around the waist, threw him over my shoulder like a sack of grain and scooted as fast as I could over the downed tree.

If he had put up a fight he would have sent both of us tumbling onto the rocks below. He didn't have time to react. His inebriation worked in my favor.

We made it to the other side before he had time to kick up a fuss. When we were safely across, I set him down and told him to grab onto my belt once again.

In another five minutes of stumbling behind me, we arrived at the trailhead where I found a half dozen cars parked along the road shoulder.

I asked him to identify the car he came in. He staggered from one vehicle to another, grabbing onto mirrors, leaning on fenders, trying to look inside for clues. Eventually he settled on one he told me looked like his friend's car.

I tried the back door. It was unlocked. I asked him for his license, put him in the back seat of the car and wrote him up a summons for fishing on closed waters. I tucked the citation inside his jacket and told him to just stay put and take a nap.

He nodded. I saw his eyelids flutter and close and his head fall to his chest.

I sighed, turned and hightailed it back into the woods and down to the stream. I managed to catch a few more guys before the sun came up.

I've always wondered if that drunk fellow chose the right car that night. If not, I bet whoever owned that car never left their car doors unlocked again.

But probably the strangest night I had working smelt runs was another adventure with Warden Greg Maher.

This time we were working a stream off Lambert Lake in Washington County, which was open to smelt fishing, but with a two quart limit.

That meant we had to be certain an angler was over the limit before identifying ourselves.

That's not easy, because not only was it night, but people were pretty smart about hiding their catch too.

Even if they weren't cheating, some people just didn't want to let other folks know just how good the fishing was in their honey hole. Maybe they intended to try again here the next night or next year in the same spot. Discretion was part of the game.

The pails people carried were most often a solid color plastic—impossible to see through, especially at night.

So, I had to get right up alongside people a lot of the time, to see what they actually had in their bucket or at least to get an idea of how many times they dipped and dumped fish into their bucket.

If I jumped the gun and was wrong, it could mean I'd had wasted the entire night at a location.

Because as soon as I said, "Warden! Stop right there and show me your bucket," people scattered like ruffed grouse up and down the water.

A dozen or more people might fish together on a stream. Every one of them was listening for any sign of trouble. Even for the many people who were fishing legally, many of them still didn't want to have a conversation with a warden.

So, there wasn't much worse than identifying yourself as a warden to someone you thought had taken too many smelt, and then discovering the angler had a valid license and less than the two quart maximum in their pail.

Whether or not any of the people you stopped and talked to were violating the law, you could be certain every one of them would warn anyone headed down to the water, "Watch out! There's a warden down there!" and the ones without a current fishing license would turn tail and drive away fast.

The best way to work a smelt run was get elbow to elbow with the other anglers—to look like one of the herd.

That meant I had to lose the clean cut woods cop look and find my inner long haired, slightly less ambitious, beer drinking smelt thief.

To do this, I borrowed a woman's wig from Greg's wife, Sue. The wig sported synthetic brown hair that tumbled down to just below my ears. No need to comb it. The more mussed up the better.

Wearing the wig was a little hot and itchy at times, but not bad on cold Spring nights. It got worse when I capped the wig with a felt crusher hat to complete my disguise. When I did this, my noggin had more than double its usual insulation.

Along with the wig, I wore a beat up jacket, jeans and waders.

Under this outfit I was wearing my uniform, complete with badge, radio and my sidearm. But in the dark, no one could tell who I was.

To top it off, I carried a beer can, which I dipped into whatever water I could find on my way to the stream. I'd lift it to my lips every now and again and pretend to drink, while making certain I didn't swallow any of the contents.

A case of Giardia was not on my wish list.

The beer made me look the part and it was also handy as an excuse to walk off into the woods after explaining, "Unh, 'scuse me, I gotta take a leak. I'll be right back."

Anglers with a taste for beer never questioned my retreat as they too were well acquainted with the demands of the human bladder following significant beer consumption. They'd just nod and get back to their fishing.

Slipping off into the brush allowed me to quietly radio Greg back at the trailhead.

We had a system where I could spot the folks I believed had taken too many fish or were acting so jumpy they were indicating they didn't even have a fishing license.

I'd give Greg descriptions of the suspects when they left the water and headed back to their vehicles under the pretense of answering Nature's call.

Greg would step out of the bushes in uniform and stop and chat with those anglers I suspected of breaking the law.

But a beer can, long hair and regular guy clothes weren't sufficient to pull this charade off. I also had to fish.

So I had my own net—modified slightly, of course.

Because, if the smelt were running good it would take only 20 minutes to get a two quart limit. If you really worked at it, probably even less time.

I needed to be on the stream for hours
watching people come and go.

I had to dip but not catch a lot of fish, to give
myself a reason to stick around and watch
everyone around me smelt fish.

So, I cut a hole in the bottom of my net—a big
one. And every time I lifted my net to fill my
pail, all but the unluckiest smelt would slide out
of the hole and back down into the stream.

Dressed the part, sporting long hair and
hoisting a beer to my lips now and again, none
of the other anglers gave me a second look.
I fit right in.

Guys didn't care to see how many smelt I was
catching. It was too dark to be nosy. They were
intent on netting their own fish and going home.

I was golden—until I ran into this woman.

Greg and I had teamed up to monitor a smelt
run along a brook leading into Lambert Lake in
Washington County.

This stream was open for smelt fishing, but we
had been advised it might have to be closed in
the future due to low numbers. The experts
wanted to know how much poaching factored
into the reason the annual smelt run here had
fallen off so dramatically.

We used the same approach that had worked for us many times before. Greg hid where he could watch people leave and return to their vehicles, while I had the honors of feeding him information from down on the brook.

I'd been on the water a couple hours, when a woman, maybe 40 years old or so, noticed that despite what appeared to be a good deal of effort on my part, I didn't appear to be catching much.

Most guys will dip, dart around in the water and dump their catch into their pail and once they are satisfied with their catch, they leave without so much as a howdy.

Most guys don't even say a word to one another, unless they are family members comparing pails.

But this particular dipper was as chatty as a minister welcoming a new parishioner.

I had seen her watching me out of the corner of my eye for a half hour or so. I was hoping she would just fill her pail and leave.

No such luck.

She sidled on over to me and said, "How are you doin', Hon?" and instead of just standing back and introducing herself, she pulled out her flashlight and shone the beam square into my pail.

She seemed to want my job.

I yanked my bucket back, turned a disinterested shoulder towards her and grunted, "Uh, not bad."

But she'd seen my pail had less than a half dozen fish in the bottom.

Her head shot up and she looked at me with her mouth open.

"Golly, you haven't got hardly any smelts," she said with a shocked look on her face.

I tried to not let her rattle me and replied, "I'll catch up in a bit." And I bent down again to stick my net in the water so she wouldn't notice anything was wrong with it.

"Well, your feet will freeze before you get enough for a meal, at the rate you're going," she said.

I took a step up river thinking she will take the hint and just leave me alone.

But she follows alongside me, reaches out and says, "Let me see your net. Maybe there's something wrong with it."

Well, what could I do? I had to play along.

"Uh, here," I said, lifting my net out of the water. She trained her flashlight beam on the net.

In two seconds, she figured it out.

"Well, lookee here! This is your problem," she said, pulling the net bottom up within six inches of my nose. "You've got a big ole hole right here in the bottom of your net. No wonder you ain't catchin' the smelts."

She shook her head back and forth and looked at me like I was an exceptionally pitiful doofus desperately in need of her assistance.

Maybe, I reminded her of someone in her family or maybe it was that famous maternal instinct. Maybe she was hitting on me. I don't know.

But she insisted on taking me under her wing.

"Here, let me help you catch some fish," she said. "We'll use my net, okay? It works great."

And she bent over and started scooping up smelt while asking me all these questions. She wanted to know where I was from, was I married, where I lived, if I had any kids.

I told her I was married with four kids and I was just visiting here from Connecticut and a friend had told me about the smelt run, so I thought I'd try it.

"Oh!" she said. "I lived there for awhile. Where in Connecticut are you from, Honey?" she asked me.

"Providence," I said.

She looked at me like I was even dumber than she thought. "Providence?" she repeated, trying to place the town on the map in her mind.

I realized I'd just screwed up. I was thinking of Rhode Island. I had to come up with something fast.

"Yeah," I said looking at her all innocent. "It's just a little bitty place."

"Oh," she said, turning her attention back to the stream. When she went back to dipping, I breathed a sigh of relief.

"Now, you hold your pail out like this, out in front, okay? So I can get them all in there for you," she said.

I felt like I was five years old and my mother was teaching me how to knock on doors and hold my bag open to be filled with treats from strangers on Halloween.

She dipped and dumped, took a step sideways, then dipped and dumped some more—over and over—until my two gallon bucket was full of smelt.

Oh my. Here I am paid to protect the fishery and instead I'm contributing to its demise thanks to her help.

This was not good. What to do?

I say, "Geez, that's an awful lot of fish. That's way over the limit, isn't it?"

She grinned at me and winked like I was her favorite nephew and she wanted me to have a bigger slice of strawberry rhubarb pie than the other boys.

"Ah, you'll be all right," she said with a big smile. "You need enough for a meal for you and your wife and kids."

"Well, I think I had better get outta here fast. I don't wanna get caught," I said looking up and down the stream.

"Caught?" she asked me, like I was crazy. "Who's gonna catch you?"

"A warden," I said looking her square in the face with my eyes wide and my head turning, acting all nervous and twitchy.

She laughed hard, shook her head and smiled like I was telling her I was afraid of Bigfoot coming out of the bushes.

"Pfffft! There's never any wardens come up here!" she said trying to put my mind at ease. "They're all out chasing deerjackers. Wardens don't care about a few little fish," she told me.

"Well, I'm way over the limit," I said, "and my luck hasn't been that great lately."

I start doing the antsy dance and looking up the trail.

"I think I had best be gettin' outta here fast," I tell her.

"Well, you're headed home with a nice mess of smelt for your family," she said smiling with great satisfaction at having helped me.

I felt like a guy who volunteers to help wash dishes at a church supper and when the minister finds a big tuna casserole no one has touched, she tells me to take it home to the family.

I guess me telling her I had four kids to feed had made an impression on her.

And after seeing the hole in my net and me telling her Providence was in Connecticut, maybe she was convinced my kids would starve if I were their sole breadwinner.

She appeared willing to clean out this stream to help me feed my imaginary brood.

I looked at my bucket full of smelt and said, "Wow. I would have been here all night if it wasn't for you."

There was a double meaning in this last statement, of course. Was Greg listening in?

I had gotten myself all dressed up for a busy night of undercover work on this stream and instead, it looks like we are going home early.

If I dump the smelt or behave in any way like I'm not thrilled to have them, my cover is blown.

This good Samaritan is sending me off the water and up the trail.

My new fishing buddy flashes a huge smile at me and says, "I'm just happy to have helped you. You come on back and see me if you need some more."

I nod and lift my pail to my hip and scuttle across the stream.

I hear her call after me, "Be sure to sew up that hole in your net when you get home, okay?"

I shake my head and run up the trail to where Greg is hiding.

I turn myself into my partner.

Greg whistles in awe when he sees my haul —I'm many quarts over the lawful daily limit.

"Providence, Connecticut?" he whispers.

"You think maybe you need to work on your geography?" he teases me trying not to laugh out loud.

I shake my head and say, "I know! I know! That lady had me shook. I sure didn't expect her to get all helpful like that!"

There's no putting the fish back in the water. It's time to bag this night's sting operation and move on.

"Well, let's not let them go to waste," Greg says. "I know some people who can use them."

I yank off my hat and wig, slide out of my waders and we walk to Greg's cruiser and remove the parachute hiding it back in the bushes.

Greg and I called on four different households that night. They were all older Mainers who, for various health reasons, could not smelt fish anymore.

You would have thought Greg and I were Santa Claus. When these folks opened their front door and saw two wardens standing there with a small bucket of fresh caught smelt just for them, it literally brought tears of gratitude to their eyes.

Of course, all the recipients had lots of questions for us.

They wanted to know where we had found the run, how many anglers were on the stream, if the smelt were running like in years gone by, how many poachers we'd caught and if any of them had managed to get away...

Greg did me a big favor. He just smiled and asked about how their kids and grandkids were doing, to change the subject.

But at every stop, someone would say, "I just wish I could thank that poacher personally," look us both in the eye and laugh heartily at their joke.

I winced every time.

I just couldn't bring myself to tell them the poacher to thank was me.

"I really don't want to look.
I was having a nice morning
until Basil pulled this stunt."

BRAGGING OR LYING

My brother in law, Basil Durrell, was well known to many in the greater Franklin County area of Maine. Basil worked many years as a salesman for a big lumber and home supply outfit there. Just about anyone in a range of 60 miles wanting to remodel or build sought Basil's sage counsel.

He had a wealth of knowledge on everything from kitchen cabinets to garage door openers. He saved his frugal neighbors both time and money.

But it wasn't just his sales skills that made him successful. Basil was also fun to be around. He loved to laugh and joke.

When Basil and I got together, we would have so much fun catching up on the news sometimes we'd lose track of what we were doing.

Take, for instance, the Sunday Basil and I decided to head out from Farmington to Clearwater Lake to do some ice fishing, a distance of about six miles.

It was just after dawn, with a north wind cold
enough to make your nose run and the snot
freeze in your moustache like walrus tusks.

We wouldn't last long standing out on the ice
jigging for our supper.

But no worries, Basil and I had built a
new shanty. Nothing fancy about it—some
plywood and a tin roof and a couple of pieces
of plexiglass caulked and screwed to the
particleboard siding for light. But it would keep
us out of the wind and that's what mattered.

Rita threw a few sandwiches together for us and
filled thermoses with hot coffee. I kissed her
goodbye and Basil and I went out into the cold
to load the shanty. Basil was towing a trailer
behind his Scout.

Of course, the rope had been left coiled on the
bed of the trailer and it was stiff with frost. It
was almost like a magician's trick rope—where
they take a soft loop and toss it into the air and
presto—the rope stands up straight.

I shook the snow from the line and noticed it
was frayed in a few spots, but we weren't going
far and I figured it would hold.

Basil stood on the passenger side of the trailer
and I stood on the driver's side and we tossed
the cord back and forth to one another, lashing

the shanty down. We were more focused on who had done what to whom and story telling than the task at hand.

But between the two of us, we had probably tied down 1,000 loads before.

It's not rocket science. What can go wrong, right? When I saw I was literally just about at the end of my rope, I shouted, "I'm good on my side. Are you all set over there?"

Basil shouted, "Ayup. Good." Then he added, "Hey, why don't you drive my Scout today? I really think you'd like it!"

I snugged the final foot of cord in a half hitch twice, shouted, "Okay, let's go!" and the two of us ran like kids to the front of the Scout and jumped into the cab—Basil in the passenger seat and me in the driver's seat.

I cranked the heat to high, shifted into first and we headed down the road with me doing my best not to miss any gears. Basil poured himself a cup of coffee and continued telling me stories in between sharing the many virtues of his beloved Scout.

We were less than a mile from the lake, when the front end of the Scout went over a big frost heave and I glanced in the rear view mirror to make certain the shanty held tight.

It was gone.

Instead of seeing a 4 x 8 particle board wall
behind me, all I saw was a 10 foot length of
frayed cotton rope snapping in the breeze above
the empty trailer bed.

I slammed my boot on the brake pedal.
The trailer bucked up like a Shetland pony
on Spring pasture. Basil's coffee cup flew out
of his hand, splashing black water from the
headliner to the dash and coating the inside
of the windshield.

His mouth open, he turned to look at me as if I
had lost my mind.

The Scout was sliding into the opposite lane.

I yanked the steering wheel hard and ran the
right front tire high up onto the snow bank,
threw the Scout into low, shut it off, released my
seatbelt and leaped out the driver's door.

Basil was trapped like I'd just parked the Scout
inside an igloo.

Did I think the disappearance of the shanty was
an optical illusion of some kind?

Maybe the shanty was playing games with me
and just hiding or the disappearing shanty trick
was done with mirrors?

I stood there dumbfounded. Our shanty was
gone.

I craned my neck and squinted back down the
road looking for it.

Nothing.

I picked up the length of loose cotton rope.
It was frayed at the end, like it had snapped
or been worn through with a dull blade.

It struck me that running a rope over the sharp
edges of a metal roof might not have been the
best idea. Could be banging through potholes
and frost heaves might have sawed the cord in
half.

Or maybe the wind on the shanty was just too
much for the load bearing weight. Another good
theory.

I decided I needed to forget wondering why the
shanty had up and deserted us, and focus on
where it had gone.

I coiled the rope and tied it in a figure eight to
the front rail so it wouldn't wrap around the
axle, then ran and jumped back into the Scout
cab.

Basil was mopping up the dash with a mitten,
shaking his head and trying hard not to laugh.

"Basil, when was the last time you checked on the trailer?" I asked.

"Geez, Parker, I don't know. A long time ago. I figured you were watching it," he said sheepishly. "I'm sorry."

"Well, I should have been looking too," I admitted. "But we gotta hurry and go back and find it. I just hope it is still in one piece."

I drove a few hundred yards down the road until I could turn the Scout and trailer around safely. Then we headed back towards Farmington in a hurry—craning our necks like hungry geese in search of a cornfield the bears hadn't yet picked clean.

We rode in silence, our fingers crossed, hoping no one had slammed their vehicle into the building. It was so early, not even the churchgoers would be on the road yet. That was a plus.

We drove almost the entire way home before we finally found the shanty. It never made it past the first sharp right turn.

Basil spotted it first. "There it is!" he said pointing. "Doesn't look bad at all."

I pulled the Scout over and put on the four way flashers and Basil and I both jump out to investigate.

We did indeed get lucky. The snow acted like
a pillow and saved the shanty from serious
damage. Other than the tin roof being bent up
some where it smacked the snow, it was fine.

Basil and I shake our heads and laugh at
our good fortune. Then he runs back to the
Scout to dig around for more rope. As every
backwoodsman knows, you can't carry too
much rope or tow chain.

We wrestle the shanty back onto the trailer and,
this time, we pay more attention as we tie it
down.

When we ran out of rope the shanty looked like
a fly wrapped in a deranged spider's web. It
wasn't pretty, but it wasn't going anywhere.

"You still want me to drive?" I ask Basil.
"Sure!" he says. "You're doing fine."

So, I turn the Scout around once again and, for
the second time this morning, we head for the
lake.

I slowed down a bit on this second trip. I had
a sneaking suspicion my driving might have
contributed to the shanty jumping off the trailer.
It was probably scared.

We made it to Clearwater Lake a lot later than
we had planned, but there was still plenty

of good ice to choose from. Basil and I even managed to catch a few fish that day.

But from Basil's perspective, the best part of the entire trip was losing the shanty. He loved to tell that story at family gatherings. And I have to admit, it was a good one.

And Basil was right about the Scout too. I liked it so much I bought one for myself a few years later.

But our shanty mishap pales in comparison to the premeditated prank Basil pulled later.

It was a balmy Saturday in June and I had a welcome day off, as did Basil.

We had arranged to do some errands together. Rita and I were at her mom's house. Basil swung by to pick me up in his work truck. He often used Saturday mornings to check on the progress of his clients' home construction projects. This way, he could keep cabinets and plumbing fixtures and more, flowing to the job site as the crew needed them. It was all part of Basil's great customer service.

We made a few stops, he took some notes and I was happy to just ride along and watch the scenery.

Around 10 am, Basil turns up a road I don't recognize. He drives a quarter mile or so and pulls into a gravel driveway leading to a modest single story home.

This stop wasn't on our list. There was no exterior construction underway that I could see.

"What's up?" I ask him.

Basil grins and throws his truck into park, kills the engine and says, "I want you to meet someone."

I shrug and say, "Okay," and get out of the cab. I follow a few paces behind Basil as he climbs the front steps.

Basil knocks on the screen door, shouts, "Anybody home?" and when we hear a shout, he opens the door and walks inside and motions for me to follow.

It is clear he knows these folks well enough to just stroll in.

We walk through a tidy living room, past the television, past a sleepy cat curled up on the couch, to the kitchen. We find a couple about our age—late 30s—sitting at the kitchen table having coffee and reading the newspaper.

When the man of the house sees Basil, he gets a big smile on his face and says, "Well, look what the cat dragged in, Ruth!"

I look down and see there indeed is another cat—this one gray with a white muzzle and paws—wrapping itself around Basil's ankles as he reaches for a chair and sits down.

The wife looks up from her coffee, smiles and says, "What are you up to today, Basil?"

It strikes me as odd Basil doesn't immediately introduce me to his friends, but I don't say anything. I pull another chair out from around the table and sit down and listen to the three of them exchange pleasantries.

The gray tomcat moves from Basil to me. I bend down to give it a chuck under the chin for something to do.

Basil and the couple are busy chatting and laughing. I have one ear on their conversation and the other listening to the cat purr as he wraps himself around my legs.

After a couple of minutes, Basil asks, "So, Raymond, how's your fishin' for brookies going? Havin' a good year so far?"

Now, when the subject of fishing and hunting come up, I get interested. I mean, it's my job to be interested. Irregardless of whether I am in uniform or not, day off or not, I perk up.

I keep my head down, but I'm listening.

The fellow responds with a big smile, "Sure am! I caught a dozen brook trout just t'other day. It's goin' real good!"

At the time, anglers were limited to five brook trout daily and each fish had to measure at least six inches from nose to tail.

I shoot a look sideways at Basil but I don't say a word. He doesn't acknowledge my glance.

Basil breaks into a big grin and nods as if he approves of his pal having caught more than twice the daily limit.

Raymond smiles back even bigger, then takes a satisfying long pull on his coffee cup and sets the mug down, like it was a shot of 30 year old Bourbon.

Our host believes Basil is duly impressed with his fishing prowess.

But I know better. Basil is up to something. The homeowner obviously has no idea who I am or he would never boast about breaking the law.

I feel my stomach sour. I think of all the ramifications here.

I know if this fellow is a pal of Basil's, it could be he's just bragging to impress Basil, who—truth be told—is no slouch at stretching the truth himself.

I tune out the purring cat and lift my head a few inches so I can hear better. I'm still looking at the floor, pretending I'm not much interested in this conversation.

Basil doesn't let his pal's boast go by unchallenged.

"Oh, come on, Raymond," Basil says and rolls his eyes. "You didn't catch a dozen brookies in one day."

Basil shakes his head and tosses in a little "pshaw" at the end.

Raymond's smile turns to a frown and his back stiffens like Basil had spritzed cold water in his face.

"Well, I sure did catch a dozen trout in one day," he says again.

"Naaah. I don't believe it," Basil says and shakes his head, flat out accusing our host of lying. And he doesn't stop there.

"Raymond, you couldn't catch a dozen trout in one day if your life depended on it," Basil says leaning in across the formica table top and grinning smugly.

I'm squirming inside, thinking, "Basil, you just called our host a liar at his own kitchen table, in front of his wife who poured you a nice cup of coffee. Worse, you are lining up this guy to be cited by a game warden. What in the world is wrong with you? This isn't fair."

But I keep my mouth shut. As uncomfortable as this situation is, I have a job to do if indeed this guy is poaching and I can prove it.

I glance up at the wife. Her welcoming smile is gone. She's pursing her lips and suddenly very interested in the design on the side of her coffee cup, although I would bet she's been using that mug daily for a decade.

Raymond shifts his weight in his wooden chair. The spreaders creak a little as he shuffles his slippered feet beneath the kitchen table. I see the color rising in his cheeks and the cords of his neck tighten above the frayed collar of his Red Sox T shirt. His open hands close into fists.

Basil sits quietly waiting for Raymond's response, a sly smile on his face.

His sneer would have prompted some fellows to leap right across their kitchen table and grab Basil by the throat.

Good thing it's before noon and Basil's challenge is taking place in a kitchen and not a barroom, I'm thinking to myself.

99

Raymond glares at Basil and says slowly, "Yes, by gar, I sure did catch them fish, every single last one of them!"

He slams a fist on the table for emphasis. The teaspoon beside his coffee mug jumps and the table rocks.

The cat scoots out of the kitchen.

The wife has had enough too. She stands up and carries her coffee cup and saucer to the kitchen sink in silence. Then she turns on the faucet and starts washing dishes.

I weigh my options.

Raymond has just admitted to catching seven fish over the daily limit. Of course, I hadn't seen him do it though. I have no physical evidence.

Raymond and Basil stare across the table at one another like two jumpy gunslingers at a poker game. It's like Basil just accused Raymond of palming a card.

And he just won't back off. He shakes his head again and says, "Nope. Sorry, Raymond. I'm not buying it. Not you. Not on your best day. No way."

Raymond's neck bulges bigger and now his eyeballs pop too. His knuckles show white.

Raymond leans in until he is less than 18 inches from Basil's nose, like he is going to pop Basil in the mouth. He glares at Basil.

"I'm telling you the God's honest truth!" he says, raising the ante.

The two men look at one another in silence. Raymond's eyes are black and angry. Basil continues to smirk. The only sound comes from the wife washing the breakfast dishes.

She is not making a move to stop the two of them from arguing. Maybe she's used to these two bickering like brothers.

"You still don't believe me?" Raymond says to Basil—incredulous.

Raymond pushes his chair back from the kitchen table, leaps to his feet and says, "Okay, then. I'll show you, Basil! Follow me."

He sputters angrily and storms towards a door just off the kitchen.

With our host's back to us and his wife facing the kitchen sink, Basil sees the coast is clear for him to give me a sign. He stands up from the table, shoots a quick glance over at me, grins like a polecat and winks.

He is in his glory.

I scowl at him, but I don't say a word.

I'm shocked Basil would play such a mean
trick on a friend and put me in a rotten spot
too. I may have to give our host a citation.

Raymond opens the door and flips the
light switch. We're standing in the pantry,
surrounded by neatly arranged shelves stocked
with canned goods, cleaning supplies and a
chest freezer.

Raymond glares at Basil, twists the freezer's
latch, lifts the lid and pulls out a plastic milk
jug stuffed full of frozen brook trout—just their
tails are sticking out.

With ingenious Yankee frugality, Raymond
has cut the top quarter off a gallon plastic
milk jug, left the handle intact, put the
deceased brookies in nose down, filled the jug
with water up to the cut, then put the jug in
the freezer. When you want a fish dinner, just
pull the milk jug out and let the jug thaw in
the sink.

Basil leans in to take a closer look at the jug,
while making certain not to block my view.

I really don't want to look. I was having a nice
morning until Basil pulled this stunt. But, of
course, duty calls. I have no choice but to look
at the evidence.

Basil stares intently at the jug loaded with forked tails. He pretends to have trouble counting them all.

"Go ahead, Basil," Raymond says, "Take a good look! You want me to count 'em for you too?"

Raymond lifts the jug closer to the overhead light, so Basil can get a better look at the brookies. Basil helps Raymond. He holds the freezer lid open.

Raymond tilts the icy pail closer to Basil and says, "There! There's proof! I caught a dozen of them." And when he figures Basil has seen it long enough, he lowers the jug back into the freezer.

Basil still isn't satisfied. "A block of ice?" he says and shrugs his shoulders. "What does that prove?"

"Well, how do you figure all them trout got froze together if'n I didn't catch them all at the same time?" Raymond says, about spitting nails. "Hunh? Hunh? You tell me how!"

Raymond is doing a crack job of incriminating himself.

Basil shoots a glance at me. He has given me plenty of time to count the fish tails sticking out of the ice block. I can tell Basil figures

Raymond's last admission should about wrap this case up.

Basil purses his lips and concedes defeat.

"Well, Raymond. You do make a good point about the ice. I guess you must be telling the truth. I agree, you must have caught all those fish in one day."

"Well, yer durn tootin' I did," Raymond says, beaming to have at last proven his case. "Yup, I caught all them brookies on the same day."

"Ayup. Ayup. I see that now," Basil says and nods. "I guess, you are telling the truth."

Raymond smiles like a second grade boy who has recited a poem on the school stage without forgetting a single line.

He slams the freezer lid shut in triumph.

"Of course, I'm telling the truth, Basil. It's the God's honest truth, I caught all them fish in one day," Raymond says.

Satisfied he has convinced Basil at last, Raymond turns to lead us back to the kitchen.

Basil stops him, saying, "Oh Raymond. I'm sorry. Where are my manners? I don't think

I introduced you to my brother in law here.
This is Parker Tripp."

Raymond turns towards me, puts his right
hand out and we shake. "Pleased to meet you,"
Raymond says. I nod, but I don't say a word.

"You've heard me talk about Parker before,
Raymond," Basil says with a grin. I can
see Raymond wracking his brain trying to
remember the name.

"He's a game warden," Basil says and keeps
smiling.

Raymond gets a funny look on his face, like
he just ate a piece of candy given to him by a
friend and now that friend is telling him it was a
chocolate covered cricket.

"Don't say that, Basil!" Raymond says, like
someone just asked the Devil to pay his home a
visit. "That's not funny."

"I'm not kidding," Basil says feigning innocence.
He turns to me and smiles and says, "Go ahead,
Parker. Show him your badge."

I don't like being used as the bad guy here. But
I reach into my back pocket, pull out my wallet,
flip it open and there it is—gleaming gold shield.

Raymond's face goes white. His jaw drops.

There is fear in his eyes.

He looks up into my eyes to see if maybe this is all some sort of joke and I'm going to tell him my badge is fake.

I don't speak and I don't smile.

Raymond looks over at Basil. Basil is clearly relishing seeing his buddy in the early stages of a heart attack.

I feel bad for Raymond. There's a part of me that wants to take Basil outside and shake him.

Both Basil and I wait to hear what Raymond says next.

There's dead silence for a count of three.

Then Raymond breaks into a kinda fake chuckle, shifts back and forth nervously on his feet, hikes up his pants, raises his head, juts out his chin and says, "Aw, gee whiz, Basil. You know me. I'm one of the biggest liars in all of Franklin County. Always was and always will be."

Raymond looks over at me and adds, "It took me three days to catch all them brookies."

Then he follows this with a hearty "Ha Ha Ha" and looks hard into my eyes to see if I am buying it.

I am some impressed with Raymond's ability to think on his feet. He even got the math right.

He had just wriggled his way out of me writing him a citation. Without me having seen him catch the fish, even with his earlier confession, it would be about impossible to make this case in court. Frozen all together in a jug or not, someone else might have caught some of those fish.

Raymond could easily argue he was just trying to impress Basil with a fisherman's tale.

His fun over with, Basil looks down at his watch.

"Oh geez, Raymond. It's getting late. Parker and I gotta get going. We've got a lot of errands to do today," he says.

Raymond nods in silence and the relief on his face shows big. I'm pretty certain he believed he was two seconds away from being led out of his home in handcuffs.

Basil steps through the doorway back into the kitchen. I follow. Raymond flips the light off and closes the door.

The three of us walk through the kitchen, through the living room to the front door. I look about for the lady of the house to thank her for the coffee, but she's disappeared.

Raymond opens the front door and Basil and I step onto the front stoop. I see Raymond's face is pale. He's walking like he just got hit in the head with a 2 x 4—stunned.

He's wondering if I am going to come back and arrest him.

Basil takes two steps and then stops and turns. He can't resist rubbing it in just a little more before we drive away.

"Hey, Raymond, anytime you want to show a warden your illegal catch, you just give me a call and I'll bring Parker over," he says.

I shoot another dirty look at Basil.

He barely makes it to the driver's seat before he collapses in paroxysms of laughter.

"Did you see the look on his face?" Basil says to me, gasping for air.

I climb into the passenger seat and shut the door. I'm not laughing. "Basil, that was a mean trick to pull on your friend," I say.

Basil is hooting. Tears stream down his cheeks. We can't leave the driveway because Basil can't see to drive.

I know from experience poor Raymond has run

back to his freezer and is tossing all his frozen
fish and meat out, wanting to get rid of any
and everything I might question him about if I
return with a search warrant.

"Come on, Basil, let's get out of here," I say.
"You're giving your friend a heart attack with us
still here in his driveway."

Basil finally turns the key and we leave. He
gloats all the way home. He considers this one
of his best gags ever.

Whether Raymond was bragging or lying—or a
little bit of each that day—I never did find out.

I only knew I didn't have the evidence I needed
to make a case.

And, after mulling it over, I decided it didn't
matter.

Whether Raymond was bragging or lying about
his catch, I knew he would never—ever—do it
again.

"I step out onto the deck and shout
at the top of my lungs towards the house and
wave my arms in a clear distress signal."

Captain Calamity

 s a warden in the 1970s and '80s, we worked with some pretty basic watercraft, to put it kindly.

Recoil starts on small outboard engines fitted to 14 or 16 foot open aluminum hull boats. Nothing to shade you from the sun.

Patrolling Maine's ponds and lakes on cloudless summer days in uniform, we'd bake like a Presque Isle potato wrapped in aluminum foil.

And God forbid a thunderstorm whipped up, because the folks you were watching might just have to rescue you. Even if you didn't get swamped before you made it to shore, you could count on getting soaked along with all your gear.

So, when I was promoted to Sergeant and moved to magnificent Moosehead Lake, I decided this was my opportunity to buy a big, comfortable boat for our family to enjoy on my days off.

We rented the pilot's house at Fish & Game headquarters there. A dock came with it.

I was sitting on my own little piece of water connecting me to over 45 miles of sweet shoreline, some of the best in New England.

It just seemed a shame to spend my free time traveling in a tiny, shiny tub.

Lucky for me, my wife enjoys the outdoors as much as I do, so it wasn't hard to convince Rita to make the financial commitment. We agreed with careful budgeting, we could make it work.

It was the end of the boating season with big discounts being offered.

I visited several marinas with our budget in mind. There were a lot of things to consider, in addition to the price tag.

I wanted a boat we could use to entertain friends and family during the day and then enjoy at night—rocked to sleep by the waves in below deck bunks.

It didn't take me long to find some tempting deals.

I settled on a 21 footer with a cuddy cabin— inboard motor, fiberglass hull and a hatch on the foredeck.

It was one of those love at first sight kinda purchases, I guess. The boat was fast and it had style.

I had never handled anything bigger than 14 feet with oarlocks.

This cuddy cabin was massive by comparison. You could actually walk around, stretch your legs and get comfortable.

I was as happy as a Greek shipping tycoon.

It was going to be such a joy to have our very own seaworthy vessel tied up to the dock next Spring. But first, I had to live through another Maine winter.

There was a big hangar on Moosehead Lake owned by the Department, used as a base for our planes. Wildlife surveys, search and rescue operations, checking licenses in remote areas and more.

I asked and received permission to store my new boat inside the hangar for the Winter.

My spotless yacht was trailered by the dealer right from the showroom straight into storage. That stung a bit.

But the facts are when you buy a boat in the Fall in the snowy Northwoods, you save but you suffer.

What I mean is, I was like a teenager counting the days until he can get behind the wheel of

his first car. I really wanted to be at the wheel,
wearing the sunglasses, maybe even sporting a
corny captain's cap.

All Fall and Winter and on into April, I dreamed
of cruising up Moosehead Lake with Rita and
son, Brian, on the new boat.

We'd invite family and friends on board to share
in the fun.

I imagined us fishing, water skiing, gazing at all
that shoreline—and at night sitting out under
the stars watching clouds race over the moon
and listening to distant geese.

But it's a long time between October and July 4th.

I'd be sitting very still off in the deep woods
watching for poachers—a freezing rain driving
into my face, trickles of ice water soaking
through my collar, dripping down my back—
and I would comfort myself with thoughts of
being out on the water putting that powerful six
cylinder engine through its paces.

Just thinking about all the fun I was going to
have on that boat brought a smile to my face
that wouldn't quit.

Of course, no boat is ever really finished. They
are like houses. Owners want to personalize
them, add this and that.

I was no exception.

Right off, I knew I wanted to install a portable toilet, a depth finder, compass and more.

I bought boat fenders before I left the marina and a length of line to tie up to the dock along with quality wax for the hull.

As soon as I got the boat in the hangar, I began working to install the toilet—a "head" in nautical terms. With Winter coming on fast, there were days it was colder inside than outside.

I thought I did a pretty good job. I built a wooden box around the potty and anchored it to the boat floor. When I was done I was convinced it would take a tsunami to toss a guest off this throne. I even hung a shower curtain to give folks some privacy.

When deer hunting season came, the combination of work demands, short days and bitter cold combined to keep me from working more on the boat.

But in June, I was ready for the launch.

I wanted to give the hull one last coat of wax before the vessel was launched. I needed some sun to do that job, so the wax would flow easily.

I got lucky on my day off with high 70s and

plenty of blue sky. I had my new boat out in the yard sitting on the trailer just glistening —a sight to behold.

Rita was up in the house with Brian. I grabbed my can of wax and lint free rags, and set to work polishing my boat while enjoying the smell of fresh green grass.

Off in the distance someone was running a lawn mower. Black capped chickadees chirped in the trees nearby. A few dropped to low branches and tilted their heads like they were inspecting my work.

The lake was coming back to life.

I started at the bow, wiping the wax on and letting it dry, then buffing it to a high shine with my other hand wrapped in a clean, fresh cloth. I tackled the hull a square at a time, so the wax wouldn't dry too hard before I got to polishing.

I'd been at the task about an hour when I decided to lie flat on my back and inch my way down the keel—to polish the bottom of the boat.

I set the can of wax and a pile of rags within reach, lay down on my back beneath the bow and paused for a minute to smile and just admire the boat's craftsmanship.

I looked way up at the bow—admiring the

curves—and then let my eyes slowly drop towards the transom.

That's when I saw something that made my jaw drop and my heart stand still.

It was a protuberance about three inches long sticking out of the bottom of my boat.

I thought I was hallucinating at first. Maybe some little pointy pine pitch stick somehow glued itself there? I blinked and sat up to get a better look—almost smacking my head on the hull. I leaned in and looked harder.

It struck me this was an awful shiny twig—more like a piece of metal.

My blood pressure rose and my head swirled with all kinds of theories. A screw up at the factory? Or had some outlaw sabotaged my new boat?

I mean, how in the world could my brand new boat have a nail or a screw sticking out of it?

I hadn't even had it in the water yet. Who in their right mind would do such a thing?

Who wanted to sink me?

I sat up on my elbows and dug in my boot heels, got my behind a few inches off the ground and crabbed my way down beneath the boat to take a closer look at the offending object.

It was a stainless steel screw all right, sticking right out of the bottom of my beautiful boat.

Holy Mother of Neptune! This is BAAAAAAD!

Why in the world hadn't I seen this flaw at the boat shop?

Was my boat made on a Friday and the craftsmen all had beer for lunch?

What moron did this at the factory?

Was this the reason the boat was such a good deal?

Is my boat still under warranty?

I was just about to roll out from under the boat, jump up and run indoors and call the marina to give them a piece of my mind, when my years of police training finally got ahold of the reins on my runaway brain.

I began compiling a list of all the possible suspects. It ran the gamut from guys I had nabbed over the years to practical jokers.

I took a deep breath and craned my neck back to the bow and then followed the beam all the way to the transom. Then I looked back and tried to figure out the exact location where someone had boarded my boat and crawled into the cabin to perpetrate this dastardly deed.

Who had access to the hangar over the Winter?

Hmmmmmm.

It suddenly dawned on me the location of the screw was in very close proximity to where I had installed the chemical toilet six months earlier, before I was swamped with work during deer season and it was so cold you couldn't really work outdoors.

Had I lost my head while installing the head?

I never thought to check the bottom of the boat after my handiwork.

Could it be?

I rolled on out into the sunshine, jumped onto the trailer fender, clambered over the gunwale, took two big steps across the deck and slid down into the cabin.

I tore back the shower curtain and glared at the brand new toilet like it was suspect in a dastardly deed. Then I got down on my knees and began feeling around with both hands for a craftsman calamity.

It took a few seconds for my eyes to adjust from the bright sunshine to the dark of the interior.

My finger slid over a board that had split when someone drilled a bit off the mark. The screw appeared to have veered and dug deeper. I bent down and took a closer look.

Oops.

It was clear a dope with a drill had poked a hole in my boat all right—me!

My face got red. I shook my head.

With indisputable proof the diabolical fellow who vandalized my boat was me, I jumped up and ran to get my drill. Like a boat burglar with a guilty conscience, I dove back into the hatch and backed that screw out of the hull as fast as I could.

It wasn't that I thought if I got the screw out fast the hole would heal over.

I was just dreading the thought of a fellow warden or some friends dropping by to admire my new boat, maybe spotting the screw and me having to explain my monumental mistake.

If there was any upside to this major faux pas it was that I had not called the salesman at the marina to complain before further investigation.

But now, I'm looking at the hole in a brand new boat I want to launch ASAP. I've been telling everyone about it. Family and friends are eager to go for a ride.

I've gotta fix this fast.

I pop my head inside the house to tell Rita I am headed over to the marina.

She nods. She has already figured out boat ownership is synonymous with endless expense —whether or not the boat ever sits in the water.

When I walk into the shop, I casually inquire at the Service Desk about the best way to repair a fiberglass hull. The response leads me to believe the entire staff must have taken extensive sensitivity training.

These fellows all knew I'd bought a brand new boat here just six months earlier.

Still, not a one of them asked what boat I needed to patch.

I was grateful for that. I wouldn't have wanted to lie. But it sure would have been uncomfortable telling them the truth.

The guy sold me a box containing some special boat epoxy and shared a few tips on how to apply it.

When I got back home, I sat in the truck reading the instructions like it was a top secret memo. Sure, it would have been more comfortable to read the directions at the picnic table, or in the house, but what if someone stopped by and saw me?

I wasn't quite ready to tell Rita what I had done either.

I managed to mix up the epoxy, dash under the boat and fill the hole without anyone walking up and asking me why I was patching my brand new boat.

After a few days of hardening, sanding and finally finishing my waxing and polishing, the boat was ready for its maiden voyage.

Trouble was, no one had told Mother Nature. My day off was greeted by a Canadian cold front sweeping into the state. Weather forecasters predicted a retreating sun, blustery winds and maybe even the chance of rain mixing with snow in the higher elevations.

All but the most diehard anglers and complaining geese would be off the lake.

Well, I decided I didn't care. It was my day off and as long as there wasn't solid ice, I was going for it.

I'd been waiting six months for this day. July

4th was approaching fast and if no one else was out boating, well, that just meant I'd have the whole lake to myself.

Rita was inside, cleaning up after breakfast.

I grabbed my jacket and went out to the boat.

I checked the engine oil, the battery and the gas tank. I'd only put a few gallons in the tank because I wanted the boat to be light when I launched it off the trailer.

Filling the big tank would add a lot of weight. I didn't want it to bottom out at the launch.

The lake had a few ripples on it, but no waves. I was thinking the weatherman got it wrong.

I turned the key and the boat started up instantly—a vast improvement over yanking a rope pull on a tiller engine.

All six cylinders were running smooth as whipped cream on hot strawberry pancakes. Listening to the throaty purr of the engine and seeing the water churn up behind me—I was in heaven.

No more little toy boats for me. No sir. I had joined the big boys now.

I feathered down the choke to an idle, ran to the

gunwale and untied the bowline from the cleat. Then I jumped back to my station behind the wheel, pushed the lever firmly into reverse, gave her a little throttle and backed my yacht out into the open water.

I managed to do it without scraping the newly polished hull and was pretty pleased with myself.

I pulled up the boat fenders so they wouldn't blow in the wind and slid the throttle forward. The boat's bow parted the waves effortlessly.

I turned towards the broad lake, gave her more gas and imagined I was at the helm of a cruise ship.

My speed picked up and the boat began to plane.

I was grinning ear to ear like a 10 year old boy who had just taught his puppy to shake hands.

The wind in my face, the surge of the boat through the waves, the wide water possibilities and me—Captain Tripp—it couldn't be better.

I had a spectacular time putting the boat through her paces, playing with the tilt and trim, turning the boat to create a wake and then circling back and running through the waves to see how she handled rough water.

After 30 minutes of fun, I looked at the gas gauge and saw it read dangerously close to empty. I needed to get back to the dock and fast.

The wind had also picked up and what had been nearly flat water was being whipped up into some serious whitecaps.

I bent lower in the cabin and looked up.

The whole sky was an eerie orange with big black thunderheads scudding right for me.

A few sprinkles hit the windshield. I couldn't tell if the sky was spitting rain or snow.

Definitely time to tie up at the dock.

I swung the bow around and headed for home wishing I had put more gas in the tank. The big engine was nice, but it appeared to have a drinking problem. I was used to gas sipping outboards.

As I approached the house, I put the boat into neutral about 100 feet from shore and ran to toss the fenders out. With the throttle disengaged, and hardly any fuel in the tank, the boat tossed like a cork in the churned up water.

I stepped outside the protection of the cabin and got punched in the face with an icy north wind.

It brought tears to my eyes. I stumbled over to the gunwales like I was navigating shifting ice, grabbed the fender from the stern and tossed it overboard.

It came right back at me, into the boat. The wind was blowing about 30 miles an hour.

Oh boy.

I picked it up again and laid it over the side and held it against the gunwale trying to convince it to stay there. It fought like a big Muskie in the stiff breeze.

I decided to just hope for the best and pulled myself along the gunwale until I reached the bow, got my hands on the front fender and tossed it over the rail. It too, didn't want to leave the boat, and I decided to add duct tape to my list of things to carry with me next time.

I had this idea I would line the bow up with the dock, feather the throttle to a crawl, glide through the quiet blue water parallel and just a foot from the dock, then jump gracefully from the boat to the dock and tie up.

I ran back inside to the wheel and gave the boat some gas.

But the wind and the water were making me realize my exit would not go smoothly. This wasn't as simple as jumping out of a rowboat.

I had to get the bow close to the dock, cut the throttle, run through the cuddy cabin, jump out of the hatch and grab the bow line. Then, leap onto the dock and tie the line to the cleat before the wind tore the line out of my hand and carried the boat away.

It was kind of a marine version of rodeo calf roping.

I was fit and fast, but I was up against a world champion—Mother Nature.

Well, what choice did I have? I had to get this done.

I was kicking myself for not having asked Rita to come with me.

I maneuver the boat within 50 feet of the dock. I see whitecaps slapping the shore and the dock is soaked from the spray. My boat is rocking side to side and front to back—all mixed up.

I have no choice but to go for it. Pretty soon the engine will run out of gas and die. Suddenly, the warden service model of assigning us all open boats with gas sipping engines, shallow draw bottoms and oars for back up, was looking pretty wise.

That's another thing I forgot to put on board
—a paddle. In this wind with this big a boat,
I knew a paddle wouldn't save me either. But it
might help me push the bow or stern away from
smashing into the dock if the engine died.

I added paddles to my Buy This list.

I gave the boat a final shot of gas and when I got
within 20 feet of the dock, I cut the engine and
made my run.

I had my elbows out as I bounced off the cabin
like a ping pong ball towards the hatch.

By the time I got out on the deck, the wind had
pushed the boat 12 feet from the dock and I was
broadside.

I have no more control than a beetle on a torn
lily pad.

I jumped back through the hatch and raced to
grab the wheel and throttle again.

I threw the boat into reverse and backed up fast
before the boat drifted into overhanging tree
limbs and slammed into the shallows.

Then I circled about and attempted to dock again.

No way could I jump and tie up to the dock.
The wind and waves beat me every time.

I considered jumping over the side into the lake.

But the water here was deep, way over my head. Two men could not have held the bow in this gale. I knew I'd be yanked off my feet and dragged down the lake beside the boat.

If only there was someone on shore to catch the bowline.

I look around for Rita. Is she watching this show out the kitchen window?

I need my mate to get down here and be my first mate.

I circle out far enough where I hope to see her inside the house. I step out onto the deck and shout at the top of my lungs towards the house and wave my arms in a clear distress signal.

I catch a glimpse of her walking through the living room. I jump and scream louder.

She doesn't look up. She doesn't see or hear me.

If only I had an air horn to signal her.

Another good idea. I add air horn to the list of items to buy, along with a line for the stern, duct tape and a ship to shore radio. Of course, there's no need to buy any of these things unless I manage to survive this maiden voyage.

I'm 50 feet from shore bobbing like a cork.

After a half hour of shouting, waving and drifting up and down the shoreline, I was hopping mad from anger and embarrassment and hoarse from screaming into the wind.

In frustration, I grabbed the throttle and slammed it full forward. The engine roared to life, the bow shot up in the air like a killer whale chasing a seal.

I'm tossed backwards and find myself looking directly into the black storm clouds.

The prop digs a hole in the lake so deep, water spews up like a geyser over the transom and onto the deck.

The boat flew out of the hole like a witch on a broom. It was impressive power that almost knocked me off my feet.

I throttled the engine back and took a deep breath and scanned the shoreline for anyone who might be able to grab the line and help me tie up.

There's not a soul around. I'm on my own. I take a deep breath and try to dock the boat solo again.

I tried more than a dozen times. The gas gauge

fell deeper into the red zone with every futile maneuver.

The storm worsens. The wind whistles through the cabin. The waves are bigger than ever. It's raining hard, with a mix of sleet and snow pelting the roof above my head.

I know if I run out of gas I am totally out of luck—adrift. I will have no control.

I envisioned my diamond shined hull slammed up on rocks, a big gash in the side of the boat, the propeller bent and lower unit destroyed.

I feel the boat's engine begin to die.

The bow climbs a wave and it coughs because it is no longer getting enough fuel. Slide back down the wave and the engine surges forward as the last sips of gas reach the engine.

I'm done for.

It is time for this captain to make a tough call.

I point my bow at the least rocky piece of shoreline I can find, push the throttle full forward and run my prize possession—our beautiful new boat—hard aground.

"Take that, Neptune!" I scream into the merciless Moosehead maelstrom—or words to that effect—

and just before I crashed into the shore, I raised the lower unit and kill the engine.

There's no time to mourn.

I ran through the cabin, jump out of the hatch, grab the bowline, drop over the gunwales and into the shallows onto dry land and tug and tie the bowline to the stoutest tree I can find.

Then I turn and look back and shake my head.

I feel betrayed. Rita and I have invested a lot of money in this boat. I've spent a lot of time improving it.

I'm at the helm less than an hour and now here I stand with soaked socks and shoes watching the glistening hull I so tenderly polished to a high shine, grind into the rocks and sand along the shore.

I try not to let my emotions get the best of me.

Anger, embarrassment, wounded pride. All that and more are having a party in my head.

I run up to the house and tell Rita I just ran our new boat aground and I need to take the car and go buy some gas.

She looks at me like I'm insane.

Just a few days earlier I'd confessed to drilling a hole in the bottom of our new boat. Now, I just rammed the hull into the shore?

I grabbed my wallet, drove to the nearest gas station and filled two big gas cans with fuel. I stopped at a hardware store and picked up some more rope too. I realized a line on the stern would certainly help.

When the storm subsides later that afternoon, Rita helps me push the boat off the shore.

I breathe a sigh of relief seeing some scratches but no cracks or holes in the hull.

As Rita holds the bowline, I clamber aboard. She hands me the gas cans and I run to the stern and empty them into the tank.

The starter has to churn until the fuel pump feeds the engine the fresh gas. But once the engine settles into an even idle, I point the boat in the direction of our dock.

Rita stays on shore.

With the luck I've had so far, I don't want to risk our son becoming an orphan.

If this boat is cursed—or this captain—at least Rita will be around to raise him.

Once I am out onto the lake, I check the cabin thoroughly with a flashlight for any sign of a leak, then climb back up to the wheel and head over to the dock.

Rita is there waiting. She welcomes me with a big smile and a wave. I feel like a sailor who has been at sea for months coming home to his sweetheart.

The mighty waves are gone. I run out of the cabin and drop the fenders over the side. This time, they lie flat without any fight.

It appears Moosehead Lake is done giving me a boating lesson.

I run back into the cabin and aim the bow towards the dock. I give the engine a little shot of gas, then throw the tranny into neutral and once again make my run for the hatch.

When I pop out onto the deck, Rita has her arms out, waiting for me to toss her the line.

She catches the bowline expertly and snugs it to the cleat. I drop back inside, shut off the engine, run aft and am able to hand her the stern line.

While she's tying it fast, I run below one last time to check for leaks—nothing.

I breathe a huge sigh of relief and when I return to the deck, Rita climbs aboard.

We spend an hour enjoying the sound of the water gently slapping the hull, admiring the view from our plush new boat.

Too soon, it is time to leave and walk back up to the house.

I stroll to the end of the dock, turn and look back at the bow.

It's scuffed up and there's a couple big scratches I may never be able to buff out.

I shake my head and laugh at myself. Suddenly, I don't see them as flaws.

They're battle scars. I earned them.

"Instead of photos of the big bucks they'd bagged, they took photos of the warden who bagged them."

BAY STATE BRUNCH

Maine prohibits hunting on Sundays. It's been the rule for generations and despite countless attempts in the Legislature to lift the ban, it has stuck like gum to a hunting boot.

Maybe lawmakers reason Sundays off gives the critters time to go to church and hunters time to rest up, or maybe the reverse, or maybe both.

But the Sunday prohibition is especially difficult for guys who travel to Maine to hunt. There's a limited number of days to bag a buck and they are spending big bucks—of the green, foldable kind—for the privilege.

As much as it aggravates Mainers, the wait can turn the hunters from other states into a twitchy mess. Residents get to hunt on the opening day, Saturday, before having to sit on the sidelines. That gives them a little bit of an edge.

Some fellows liken the Sunday prohibition to inviting skiers to come up and spend their money but ordering them to stay off the slopes every Sunday to give the snow a rest.

Most out of state hunters will leave their jobs
as early as possible on Friday, pile into a two or
three or more vehicle convoy eager to settle into
their camps.

All along their route, Mom and Pop grocery store
owners greet these travelers with open arms
and big smiles. Cash registers ring with bonus
sales of coffee, soda, countless bags of chips
and pretzels, boxes of cookies, cases of beer,
cans of nuts. Regardless of whether a guy gets a
deer, he's going to work up an appetite trekking
through the woods in the cold.

Pulling into camp late on a Friday night, most
hunters just fall into their bunks exhausted from
the drive. Some don't even bother making a fire
in the woodstove.

Saturday is generally spent sweeping out the
camp, unloading the groceries, chopping wood
for the camp stove, getting the well pump
running or hauling water from a nearby stream,
making up bunk beds and a dozen other
household chores.

By Saturday afternoon, their work is done.
They are left to sit and stare at the woods all
around them until a half hour before dawn
Monday.

Oh sure, they can sit there with their buddies
and play card games. But they could have done

that at home. Serious hunters want to be in the woods.

It's like being five years old three days before Christmas and there are all these pretty presents under the tree with your name on them, but your parents say you can't open them yet.

The temptation to pick up a box, shake it and maybe peel back the tape to peek inside is just too much for some guys.

They can't resist sliding some shells into their pocket, throwing their rifle over their shoulder and heading into the woods.

Wardens are well aware of the temptation hunters face. It falls on our shoulders to make certain everyone plays by the rules. But to have wardens watching all the hunting camps? Well, it's impossible.

So Maine has a better way. We've got eyes in the sky.

And on this particular Sunday, I met up with fellow warden and legendary pilot, Dana Toothaker, at the Greenville Airport.

Now, flying with Dana was not for the faint of heart. A change of underwear, a barf bag and your final wishes filed with the county's Probate Court were all good things to have taken care of before you climbed into the cabin beside this ace.

Lucky for me, I had a cast iron stomach and believed I was invincible.

This Sunday, we chose to focus on the Kakadjo in what was then Warden Charlie Davis' district. Then head over near Mt. Kineo towards Warden Marilyn Kenyon's area, then to Glen Feeney in Jackman and finally to the Canadian border.

The wardens on the ground were aware of this Sunday surveillance plan. We had coordinated it in the preceding days. They were prepared for me to call them from the air with any suspicious activity.

Dana got us into the sky flawlessly and I broke out my map and compass. Together, we began scouting for camps and the chance we might even see hunters crossing open land below.

It's amazing how the woods come to life with human activity when deer rifle season arrives in Maine. Areas that hadn't seen a human for 10 months suddenly sprout mess tents, camper vans, trucks, ATVs and more. Just about anything on four wheels or rolling tracks— capable of hauling hunters in or a trophy deer out—are utilized.

I took compass readings and jotted them down in a notebook and marked up my maps. We knew which hunting camps had given us problems before and might deserve careful watching.

I let the wardens on the ground know which camps were now occupied.

I radioed whatever information I could provide to wardens that I thought might help them. It could even include the number and types of vehicles.

Gathering and sharing this information was useful not just in enforcement, but it could be invaluable if we had to track a lost hunter or get to an injured person. Maine is a big, wild state. Time is of the essence when searching for anyone here.

But it was clear skies and smooth sailing this particular Sunday. Dana and I covered a lot of miles quickly.

We headed South towards the area we call The Forks, which was Warden Lloyd Trafton's area. I called Lloyd and let him know of camps set up in his area. He responded with a cheerful "10 4" and thank you.

With plenty of fuel left, Dana turned the plane's nose toward Warden Mike Favreau's area. Mike was stationed out of Boundary Cottage, within sight of Canada.

This is remote, rugged country. Residents are fluent in both French and English, with Quebec just a stone's throw away. Some guys wouldn't like being that far out in the boonies. And sometimes people who have been in an area for generations don't exactly welcome newcomers— especially those wearing a badge.

But Mike fit right in and was well respected.

As we soared over Mike's district, I spied what appeared to be a piece of an old yellow bus, tucked back under some tall firs. It was barely visible, like the owners had worked to hide it. The tail of two pick up trucks were nearby.

All around the camp was excellent deer country—hardwood ridges that swooped down to boggy swamps. That vegetation translated into forage for hungry deer in all seasons. This was a deer Eden.

"That sure looks like a great hunting spot," Dana said to me with a nod at the bus.

"Perfect location for Sunday hunters too," I grinned. "Who would know they were there?"

Neither Dana nor I saw any fellows from the air, but we both had a sneaky suspicion something wasn't right.

I radioed Mike and told him about this remote camp and asked him to check it out.

Mike radioed me with the bad news he was way

over on the other side of his district, hot on the trail of a bunch of Sunday hunters.

"Do you mind if I check these guys out then?" I asked Mike.

"Have at it!" he replied with enthusiasm.

Dana nodded to me and grinned and began the search for a place to land the floatplane.

"How about Dole Pond?" he asked me. "Will that do?"

I looked in a direct line from the bus to the pond. The distance between the two looked like it was free of boggy ground and maybe three miles or so.

"That'll work," I said, and I set to work getting the bearings on the bus. As soon as Dana saw me stop scribbling, he turned the propeller towards the pond.

Warden Toothaker earned his wings flying the treacherous mountains of Viet Nam before becoming a Maine warden. He is renowned as a skilled and fearless master of both fixed wing planes as well as helicopters.

I can tell you from personal experience, the things Dana can get aircraft to do would scare most people to death and might even cause a few astronauts to lose their lunch.

He was revered for landing floatplanes in bodies
of water so small they are better described as
mud puddles.

Of course, it is one thing to be lucky enough
to land in a puddle without running out of
watery runway, destroying the plane or seriously
injuring your crew.

But with aviation, it is never a dead end trip.
What goes down needs to get back up into the
air and soon. There's always more cargo to carry
and passengers to fly.

So, if falling out of the sky beside Dana and
landing in a tiny puddle surrounded by steep
wooded hillsides hadn't stopped your heart, now
that you were on the ground, you could terrify
yourself worrying about the take off.

Getting out of these remote puddles was where
Pilot Toothaker really showed his stuff.

Dana had this trick I think of as a kind of
aviation version of Spin the Bottle.

He fires up the engine and motors the plane into
the middle of the puddle.

Then he winds up the engine to a scream
so loud you figure he's lost his mind. It
sounds for all the world like the engine will
blow up.

Then he starts pulling slightly on this lever and that lever and the plane starts circling over the water's surface.

With the tachometer just about pegged out and the motor begging for mercy, he circles around and around in an ever slightly bigger circle, then lowers or raises some flaps, causing the plane to get some lift under one wing.

Inevitably, the side of the plane kissing the water would be the passenger's—mine—because Dana, being the pilot, has to be able to see.

My body slams against the thin metal door, my nose is inches from the dark water racing beneath. There are some serious G forces involved when he takes off in this manner. I feel like a penny loose in a washing machine ripping through the spin cycle.

The only good news was if you did scream in terror—certain you were about to die—Dana couldn't hear you above the engine's roar.

With one ski out of the water, there would be less drag on the plane. And with the combination of power, wing flaps, lift and his passenger's teary prayers to live another day, Dana would skillfully get the plane off the surface of another unnamed Maine mud puddle.

Of course, this was often only part of the battle. Guess what you were looking at now?

Remember those mountains I mentioned earlier?

More than once, I found myself with a death grip on the dash and lifting my behind out of the seat six inches—as if that little maneuver was going to give us the extra two inches we needed to clear the trees.

I may have heard our pontoons scrape the treetops once. Dana's skills were amazing.

Lucky for us, there was no big challenge for Dana this morning. Dole Pond was plenty big enough for him to put the plane down easily.

We circled to give notice we were coming in and Dana landed the aircraft without a hitch. Then he steered the plane towards a long empty dock.

I would take my pack with my portable radio in it and call him when I was ready to be picked up. I didn't expect to be gone more than a few hours.

Dana nodded in agreement and said he would head back to Greenville to fuel up the plane and wait to hear from me.

As I jumped from the float to the pier and hoisted my pack over my shoulder, I grinned in anticipation.

If my hunch was right about these guys, I would land at their bus stop just around lunchtime.

I checked my bearings with my compass and started the three mile hike towards the camp.

It wasn't long before I topped a ridge and smelled wood smoke. It was coming from a stovepipe beneath a canvas awning stretched in front of the bus.

I leaned against a tree and watched. There was a fellow in green wool trousers and a heavy shirt wearing an apron. He was standing in front of a cook stove, with steam coming out of a big pot and a frying pan beside it.

I watched as he turned from the stove to a rough table off to his right, picked up a knife and started chopping fast and furiously. Probably onions. As any hunting camp cook knows, there are really only three essential ingredients to any meal: meat, beans and onions. Anything more is just bragging.

He seemed pretty proficient with the knife. I watched as he lifted the cutting board and used the knife to slide whatever he had diced up into the frying pan. He was definitely a guy with better than average kitchen skills.

I waited another five minutes to see if anyone came out of the bus or if he spoke to anyone.

He adjusted the flame on the cook stove, shook the handle on the fry pan repeatedly but nothing more. It appeared this camp cook was all alone.

I scanned the outside of the bus for firearms—
just in case the chef wasn't all that happy to
meet a warden.

All clear. It was time to introduce myself.
I strolled down the hill and into camp. The cook
was so intent on the stove, he didn't see me until
I was within eight feet of him. When he did
see me, he did a double take. I guess he was
expecting someone else.

I introduced myself and he reached out to shake
my hand after wiping it on his apron.

He said his name was Don and he and his buddies
were all up from Massachusetts for the week.

"To hunt?" I asked.

"Yeah, sure. These guys love to hunt," he said.
"Me, I'd rather cook and eat," he said, patting his
elf belly beneath the apron and laughing.

Then it kind of hit him he might have let the cat
out of the bag—or at least untied the string.

"Oh geez, you're a warden?" he grinned. "Oh, this
is hilarious!" he said, doubling over laughing.

Don began wiping tears from his eyes. I wasn't
sure if was from cutting all those onions, from
meeting a warden or maybe a combination of
the two.

"Where are the other guys?" I asked him.

He shook his head, still smiling, but a little embarrassed.

"Uh, well, it's like this," he said. "We all pulled in here late Friday night and they spent Saturday with me getting the camp all ship shape and then playing cards and just talking about hunting, hunting and more hunting," he said, rolling his eyes.

"But then, well, early this morning over breakfast, I guess you could say the temptation got a little too much for them," he said. "Me, I come for the quiet and to cook and just be with my friends. I love being out in the woods, but I don't hunt."

It was clear he was trying to apologize for his pals. He paused, pointed his spoon at the trees and said, "They're out there somewhere."

"They take their rifles with them?" I asked.

He pursed his lips and nodded like a kid asked to tattle on a brother who stole from the cookie jar. "They should all be back here soon for lunch. I told them I'd have lunch ready for them at noon."

Don smiled crookedly at me.

"Well, here's how I am going to do this," I said. "As each guy comes in for lunch, I am going to chat with them, take their rifle and set it aside and then get their license information. You are not to tip them off, do or say anything to warn them I'm here. Got it?"

"Oh, you can count on me, Warden!" Don said. "Honestly, I can't wait to see their faces! I won't say a word. Honest."

"Okay," I said. "I'll just take a seat here and wait."

Well, Don was the kind of fellow who didn't like to see anyone sitting at a table without something to eat.

"Hey, uh, Warden, are you hungry? You might as well eat something while you're waiting. I've got plenty of stew on the stove. I can make you a sandwich to go with it too."

Before I could say, "No thanks," Don had slid a bowl of stew and a spoon under my nose.

It would be impolite not to eat it, right?

I dipped the spoon into the bowl and while I waited for my meal to cool, I looked closer at their campsite. It was clear these fellows had put some thought into it.

They had a remote corner of the state to

themselves, the bus served as a bunk house, the attached awning protected them from the elements and they had even brought their own cook along to keep them fueled.

Don went back to the cook stove, but the silence was killing him.

"Excuse me, Warden? Do you mind if I ask you a question while we're waiting?" he asked while pushing the onions around in the fry pan with his spoon.

I looked over at him and nodded that it was okay.

"How in the world did you find us?" he asked —incredulous.

When I told him I had been dropped in by a floatplane several miles away and used my compass to guide me as I hiked in, he whistled in awe and said, "You gotta be kidding me!"

He dropped his spoon on the stovetop, leaned back, shook his head and said, "Wow! This is really something. I just can't believe you Maine wardens would take all this trouble just to check a few licenses."

I shrugged and said, "Trust me, this is nothing," and took a second spoonful of Don's stew. It was just the way I like it—thick, teeming with carrot, potato, celery and onion and tender, garlic seared beef.

"Well, I can tell you right now, your little visit is going to be the talk of my diner once I get back home! Oooooooh," he added, breaking into near hysterics once again, "I can't wait to see the look on the guys' faces when they walk up and find you here waiting."

We didn't have to wait long. Ten minutes later, there was the sound of twigs breaking underfoot from 150 feet away. A thin fellow about six feet tall strolled in with a rifle cradled in his arms. He looked a little perplexed to see a new face at camp and even more surprised when he noticed my badge.

Don said, "Warden, let me introduce you to Bob," and grinned. I shook Bob's hand, asked him to slowly give me the rifle, which he did, and I asked for his hunting license.

I emptied the rifle chamber of shells, explained the Sunday rule—which Bob admitted he knew—opened my summons book, sat back down at the table and asked him to sit across from me. I wrote him a citation.

Don brings Bob—who looks like he just ran into a fence post with his skull—a bowl of stew, a spoon and a napkin and sets it off a bit to his right so it won't interfere with our little chat.

A few minutes later, Charlie shows up and we go through the same routine. Now, Bob gets to sit back and study Charlie's facial expression in between bites of stew.

Riotous laughter breaks out around the table when Charlie's mouth falls open and his eyes pop when he spots the stranger with badge and the summons book.

Charlie joins Bob at the picnic table after I empty his rifle and set it up against the side of the bus, well out of reach.

And so it goes for the next hour, until I have five Bay State hunters laughing and shaking their heads and jabbing each other in the ribs saying, "Man, the look on your face...."

Every time a new guy would get within 15 feet of the picnic table shouldering his rifle, the others would break out in peals of laughter, point and start giggling like 12 year old boys who had conspired to put a frog in the teacher's desk.

"You've been caught Sunday huntin' by a skydiving warden," Don announced to a fellow named Andy, the last member of the crew to arrive.

Poor Andy's eyes went huge. He looked all around the camp and didn't see a stranger.

So he ducked down, jumped sideways and peered up into the trees, apparently thinking a warden was about to pounce on him from above.

He didn't think for a second he'd find a warden
elbow to elbow, seated among his pals at the
table, enjoying lunch.

When Don and Bob and Charlie and the other
guys saw Andy's reaction they about fell off the
benches they were laughing so hard.

I had never run into a group of guys like this.
Each of them was facing a hefty fine and their
license revoked for a year. Even so, there wasn't
a sourpuss among them.

They had gambled and lost and were willing to
pay the penalty.

"Who is gonna believe this one?" Charlie said
and shook his head, as I was finishing up with
Andy.

"Hey, you're right, Charlie!" Don said.
"We gotta get a picture of this!"

"Yeah, yeah. You can't leave without us getting
your picture," Don said to me. "Please? Is that
okay? I mean, otherwise, no one is ever gonna
believe this back home," he added, with the
other guys nodding in agreement.

"This is definitely strange," I thought. "But
then again, I guess it would be good for the
Department. I mean, if a photo of a bunch of
guys standing beside a warden and holding

their summonses isn't proof Maine wardens are doing their job, what is?"

So, after thinking about it a few seconds, I said, "Sure. We can do that."

And so began a mad scramble for cameras they had stashed in their trucks and daypacks.

Three minutes later, they were all set up in front of the bus, crowding around me like it was their high school graduation and I was their favorite teacher.

But instead of their diplomas each held up a summons.

And instead of photos of a big buck they'd bagged, they took photos of the warden who bagged them.

Too soon, the fun was over. They each had their citations and Don was picking up the stew bowls. It was time for me to say goodbye.

Andy spoke up as the reality began to set in. "Well boys, it looks like we'll be hunting Vermont next year. Maine won't be letting us back to hunt for a whole year."

"Ahhh, well," Charlie said, "We always have a good time here. We'll be back."

Don chimed in, "And you're welcome to join us too, Warden."

"Sure thing," Don, the cook, said. "Sunday brunch!"

They'd taken the citations so well, I was trying to think of something I could do for them when it hit me—Dana.

"I'll tell you what, Fellows. The pilot will be picking me up at Dole Pond in a little over an hour. How about I ask him to do a fly over, so you can get a photo of the plane for your friends back home too. Would you like that?"

My offer put smiles back on all their faces. They looked at one another, grinned and said, "Yeah! Great! That'll prove you actually flew in here," and "Thanks!"

"Okay then," I said. "I've got to get moving." I reached for my handset and radioed Dana as they stood in silent awe. In a few seconds, Dana was giving me the big "10 4" that he would be heading out shortly to pick me up.

The entire Bay State bunch looked at me and shook their heads, as I was a comic book hero come to life.

"Oh Man, that was soooo cool," I heard Don say as I left camp.

In a little more than an hour, Dana and I were in the air and circling over the Bay State hunters. I could see them 300 feet below us, waving with one hand and reaching up and snapping photos with the other.

Of course, Dana being Dana and hearing me go on about what really nice guys I had just met, he decided this crew deserved a close up of the two of us for their photo albums.

So, he circled back and went low—so low the fellows ran and dove for cover. I'm not so sure they got that close up shot Dana wanted to give them.

They may have just ended up with blurry photos of dirt and pine needles from his final pass. I saw two of the guys throw themselves on the ground and cover their heads.

Still, somewhere outside of Boston, I like to think there's a framed photo on a diner wall of some exceptional hunters crowding around a handsome young Maine warden—that would be me—holding up their summonses and grinning like they had just won the lottery.

I just wish I'd asked them to send me a copy.

"Would you mind taking this guy for me and checking him over good for weapons? I'm going back for another one."

Nearly Naked Nab

I t was my teenage son, Brian,
who heard the late night pot shot.

It was July. I had the weekend off and the
family and I had been enjoying it at our home
in Vassalboro.

I was asleep upstairs.

Brian was out in the yard, giving his new puppy
one more chance at watering the lawn before the
two of them turned in for the night.

I'd drifted off to sleep, lying in bed in just my
jockey shorts beneath a light cotton sheet. It was
a hot summer night with not much of a breeze.

Brian comes running up the stairs, knocks on
our bedroom door and says, "Dad! I just heard
a shot!"

He says he thinks it might have come from a
field a half mile away. I immediately recognized
the spot. It was special to a lot of people.

Parents would drive there around sunset with their little kids in their jammies, pull over and wait. The entire family would enjoy watching the does feed alongside their fawns.

To pull the trigger on a nursing doe is about as low as a poacher can go.

Trouble is my uniform, my badge, my holster— they aren't all carefully laid out next to the bed waiting for me to jump into them like a sleeping fireman called to a five alarm fire.

I'm off duty. Shorts and flip flops, sunscreen and sunglasses—that's my uniform for the next few days.

But someone should call a game warden, right?

Well, my son just did.

I throw back the sheet and race down the stairs, open the front door and run outside onto the lawn and listen.

Our driveway is set back from the main road about 75 feet through some birches.

I hear a vehicle whining in high gear, about to drive right by our home. The vehicle's headlights shine through the bare branches like shards of broken glass.

At this hour of the evening, on this little back road, to be speeding just three minutes after my son tells me he heard a gunshot?

Highly suspicious.

I run to my cruiser, throw open the driver's door, grab the keys off the dash, fire up the engine, toggle off all the lights and go chasing after whatever it is that just roared by.

It doesn't take me long to catch up with my quarry.

It's a one ton truck that had been chopped and cropped by a backyard mechanic to turn it into a tow truck. It has a crudely made boom and a low steel bed on the back. It is sporting a worn Maine license plate with mud and a crumpled rear bumper making it hard to read.

I am betting the driver is making a dash for Route 3.

As I tail the truck, I see something like a tapered stick bouncing within view and then disappearing whenever the truck slams through deep potholes.

I ride up closer to their bumper and squint, waiting for the next big bump.

It's a deer hoof.

These poachers have been so quick to throw
the deer in the bed and make a run for it, they
hadn't taken the time to tie their kill down.

The faster they drive the more the truck bounces
and bucks and the more deer I can see.

I shake my head and smile. No question I have
the right vehicle.

Now I need to figure out how many people are
riding in the cab. The boom in the back of the
truck makes it tough to see.

I drift right to peer past the wide steel
boom in the back. I feel my bare back peel
off the cruiser seat like sticky tape as I lean
forward to count heads. Sure wish I was
wearing a shirt.

It looks like a full house inside—two passengers
plus the driver.

I drop back to consider my situation. Normally,
I wouldn't hesitate to pull them over and arrest
them.

But without a weapon? Without clothes?

They have at least one rifle in there and maybe
more.

I'm a warden riding around in my underpants.

If I get pulled over by a police officer that doesn't know me, I'll have some explaining to do myself.

I try to remember what clothes and equipment my cruiser is carrying. I went down a long list of "I sure could use this right now"—pants, shirt, socks, boots, badge, weapon, wallet.

But every item I wanted went immediately under the "It ain't in here" column.

Hmmmm. I was pretty sure I had my flashlight on the seat here somewhere. I felt around and there it was. That brought a smile to my face.

Now, by any chance had I left a pair of coveralls in the trunk?

It was times like these, I envied the guys whose cruisers looked like rolling rummage sales. They always had clothes and gear to spare. You just had to keep digging.

Me, I like things neat and tidy. And this night, my good habit was about to bite me.

I sigh and try to look on the bright side. At least my jockey shorts were in top shape, with good elastic and minimal wear.

I guess my mother was right about wearing clean underwear. It had never mattered before, but, well, here I am.

After careful consideration, I decide if I keep my high beams on and run up to the driver's door fast and train my flashlight at the driver's eyes, maybe he and his buddies won't notice I'm not dressed for this occasion.

Sounds like a plan.

Did it really matter?

Nope. No way was I going to let these guys get away with this.

It was time to put my headlights on and add the blues to the mix.

For 99 percent of poachers that's enough to make them pull over.

But not this driver. He sped up.

Maybe he's color blind? Well, let me see if he's deaf.

I add the siren to my cruiser's headlights and the night piercing blues.

The truck blows a big cloud of blue gray smoke into my grill and fishtails around a corner. A cloud of dust, gravel and stones comes flying at my windshield.

I'm beginning to think I am going to need more

than my underwear and a dirty look to impress them.

I reach for the radio handset and advise the Dispatcher I am in a 10 33—police chase—with three 10 64s—night hunting suspects.

I describe the truck as best I can: a decrepit home built wrecker truck at least 20 years old, lots of rust and moving fast with three guys in the cab.

I don't request assistance. That's not my style. I just want the Dispatcher to know where I am.

I stop short of mentioning my predicament regarding my attire. I am acutely aware that a lot of Mainers enjoy sitting home next to their scanners, listening in on police, fire and rescue conversations.

The Dispatcher advises she will be sending help and I keep rolling.

My cruiser has a big advantage over the bad guys' wrecker. My wheels are built for speed, theirs is built for pulling.

I look down at my speedometer and see he is going 60 miles an hour on some of these straight sections. My rig can go twice that. No way am I going to let this truck driver outrun me.

I decided I had to do more to get their attention.
So, on the next straight section of road, I
punched the accelerator and pulled up fast
alongside the driver's door.

The driver yanked the truck's steering wheel
hard to the left and drove me off the road. My
head kissed the headliner. Saplings smacked
fenders. It sounded like a giant was shuffling a
huge deck of cards made for his hands.

I spun the steering wheel back to the right and
kept my foot on the gas to keep my momentum
and climbed out of the ditch.

Back on the road, I took a deep breath and
dropped back in behind them.

I radioed the Dispatcher and advised her to
warn whoever was coming to assist, this driver
was not being at all cooperative.

I waited for another opening, punched the
accelerator again and went after them on the
right, towards the passenger door.

The driver swerved right and I hit the brakes
and I dropped back fast. I didn't want to risk
smashing the cruiser and having them get away
from me.

I receive a radio message the state police are on
their way intending to cut these guys off.

Trouble is, the wrecker driver takes a detour.

He heads up Taber Hill Road.

We go screaming right by the Kennebec County State's Attorney's home. It's close to midnight. If he was asleep he probably isn't now. If I do my job right, he will have a new case on his desk tomorrow—three of them.

I stay on the wrecker's tail until someone inside the truck decides to up the ante.

I see an arm come out the passenger side window. Lots of times guys will try to throw out evidence. I'm not too concerned. I am looking for a landmark to mark the spot though, so I can come back later to find whatever it is they are tossing out.

But whatever is in his hand, he's not dropping it.

I hear "Pop pop! Pop pop pop!" and I realize this isn't some guy ditching a flashlight.

The far side passenger is shooting at me— probably a .22 caliber pistol.

I yank the cruiser's steering wheel to the left and drop back just far enough to put the wrecker's boom between the shooter and me.

Suddenly, that steel tripod is doing me a big favor. It may even have saved my life.

But if they think shooting at me will deter me, they've got the wrong guy.

Naked or not, nothing is going to stop me from getting these guys.

To shoot at an officer over a jacked deer?

There has got to be a lot more going on here. One or more of those guys must have outstanding warrants or be on the lam.

I see the truck's brake lights come on and then go off. The truck is slowing a bit.

I know there's a choice of unmaintained, single track lanes—Mainers call them "tote roads"—up ahead.

These guys are betting they can lose me by bulling their way up one and forcing my cruiser to get stuck.

The driver took a sharp left and headed into the woods.

I grit my teeth, slammed the brakes and dove in after them in the cruiser.

Always the optimist, I knew if my cruiser

bottomed out and got hung up, it would at least slow them down if they turned around and tried to come back out this way.

They'd have to ram my rig to get past me.

It ain't over until it's over, right?

But just in case they made it to the other side —maybe three miles away—I radioed Dispatch again.

I told her these night hunters would likely be coming out by Getchel's Corner on Route 201, if they managed to make it all the way through the woods.

"Shots fired too," I added calmly. "Warn the State Police."

I couldn't see much, but I did see a gaping mouth on the guy who had shot at me when I turned to follow them along this single track.

The driver was flying along this logging trail. Maybe the trio was concerned I might pull my weapon and shoot out their tires?

It was common practice decades earlier, but now wardens were under orders not to do it.

The driver didn't know it, but he was actually helping me by driving like a maniac.

It allowed me to race along too, and keep my cruiser from hanging up.

But it wasn't my style to just follow outlaws.

I drifted left and my headlights shone on an opportunity ahead. It's a straight stretch where —just maybe—I can squeeze on by.

My plan is to slam through the brush and alders, get ahead of the truck and turn my cruiser broadside so their truck will ram the passenger side if they refuse to stop.

I'm hoping they don't have a cow catcher on the front and enough momentum to strike my cruiser broadside and flip my car onto its roof.

Yeah, I know. I don't have a weapon or clothes or even shoes. But these guys don't know any of that.

I set my jaw, pull hard left and put the gas pedal to the floor.

Alders and sumac and weeds of all kinds are scraping, crunching, grinding and scratching my door like a box of bobcats are trying to get at me.

The wrecker is a black blur outside my passenger side window.

As soon as I see the truck's headlights in my

rear window, I yank the wheel hard to the right and slam my brakes to the floor.

I hold on tight to the steering wheel.

WHAM!

The truck slams into the rear passenger door and quarter panel and pushes my cruiser a good 25 feet sideways down the trail like a freight train.

I duck low in case they are planning to shoot at me again. I shut off all my lights and quickly radio the Dispatcher.

"I have the suspects' vehicle stopped and will be in foot pursuit," I say.

No one but me knows just how accurate that term—foot pursuit—is tonight.

I duck low and listen.

I hear a squeaky hinge on a door and feet hitting the brush. Then another door opens, closer to me—that has to be the driver.

I wait to hear a third pair of feet hit the ground. Nothing.

Maybe that guy had bailed during the time I was being broadsided?

I had to hope one of them wasn't hanging back with a weapon and a plan to shoot me.

My guess was they were all on foot and running hard.

I wasn't about to let them get away. I would chase them down. But I sure would like to be wearing some pants and shoes at least.

I ran to the trunk, popped it open and turned on my flashlight.

My jaw dropped.

My coveralls weren't in there. There wasn't a pair of boots, pants or a shirt of any kind. Nothing but jumper cables.

I shake my head. I can't believe my bad luck. Not so much as a pair of socks.

I sigh, throw my shoulders back, take a deep breath and just decide to go for it.

Experience has taught me passengers get precious extra seconds compared to the driver when they run.

I might be without shoes or clothes, but my flashlight would give me an edge.

These guys are literally running blind. I'll be able to see what's ahead.

I start running as fast as I can into the woods, ignoring the stumps, stones and brush tearing at my legs and feet.

I make it only 50 yards, when I hear the sound of glass breaking under my feet.

What? Glass? In the woods?

I stop as fast as I can but my momentum forces me to take a couple tiny steps.

It sounds like I am stepping on window panes. I hold my breath and anticipate feeling some serious pain.

I freeze and shine my flashlight down at my toes.

I've run smack dab into the middle of an aged backwoods junkyard.

There were shattered windshields, rusty car doors, wiring harnesses, tractor bodies, screws and bolts all around me like a minefield.

Of all the luck!

It's bad enough I have to run barefoot and naked through thorns and nettles and over jagged rocks and stumps.

Now, I've landed in a weedy patch hiding a farm's junkyard.

My priority is protecting the soles of my feet. Without them, I can't run. I also know I can't dawdle and tiptoe my way out of here like I'm picking daisies.

The bad guys are getting away.

I decide my best bet is to tuck and roll like they tell you to do in a house fire.

I figure even if I cut up my legs, torso or arms, I will have saved my feet. I'll still be able to run.

So, I bend low, pull my arms tight across my chest, tuck my head, hold tight to my flashlight and throw myself on the ground and roll backwards over and over and over.

In a half dozen rolls, I am on grass again and out of the broken glass and metal.

I jump up, shine my flashlight at my feet to confirm there's no more rusty metal and broken glass nearby, and begin running full tilt into the woods again.

It may sound strange, but I'm not concerned about making noise. In fact, I want the guys I am chasing to hear me crashing through the woods.

I want them so scared they run. It will make them easy to find.

Yes, I could get shot at again this way. But I never worried about getting hurt or killed, to be honest. I just figured I was immortal.

My tracking technique is to run for a dozen paces or so with my light on, then freeze, shut off my light and listen hard. If I don't hear anything after a count of 10, I start all over again.

Of course, I mix up the time I run and my listening times too. I do anything and everything to throw my quarry off, to make them show themselves.

I've been in the woods 20 minutes and covered maybe a quarter mile, when I hear something big smashing through the brush 300 yards ahead of me.

A deer wouldn't be this noisy. Neither would a bear.

I smile and run towards the sound, still alternating the light on and off pattern.

When I get within 200 feet, I shout, "Game Warden! Stop right there!"

I know he won't stop. But I also know if he keeps running in a panic in the dark, he's likely to smack his head, twist an ankle or break a leg. That works dandy for me too.

As I close in, I keep the light shining out in front and away from me. I want the guy to be blinded by the beam. I don't want him to see me barefoot in my underwear. I also want the light away from my body just in case he does shoot.

I run up within 10 feet of his stumbling backside and tell him again to, "Stop right there!"

When he doesn't, I pounce like a linebacker, knocking his knees out from under him, and slamming him face down on the forest floor.

"You're under arrest," I snarl and I pull his hands behind his back and roll onto my side and instinctively reach for my handcuffs.

Oops. I forgot. No clothes. No cuffs.

I sit the guy up and keep his eyes looking ahead. He's maybe 25 years old, reeking of alcohol and either too tired or too drunk to fight.

"Can you walk?" I ask him.

He pauses and sways, like he has to think about it a minute. Then he says in a sloppy voice, "I don't know. I might have hurt my ankle."

"Well, let me help you," I say. I stand up, then bend over and pick him up by his shirt collar and belt and get him to his feet.

"Start walking," I say.

With my left hand on his back and the other on my flashlight shining a path through the woods, we make our way back to the cruiser.

It's not hard to find. There are blue lights flashing up ahead now like a Maine lighthouse.

I walk out of the woods to find a friend—State Trooper Richard Phippen, also from Vassalboro.

I'm impressed he made it all the way up this trail in his cruiser. Not every state trooper could have done it. Dick was an outdoorsman who hunted and fished when he wasn't on patrol. If there was a trooper who could get his low riding cruiser over this trail, it was Dick.

"Hello, Dick. I'm glad to see you here," I say walking out of the woods still holding the fellow by his collar. "Would you mind taking this guy for me and checking him over good for weapons?"

Dick nods and reaches for his handcuffs. But he has a look on his face that makes me think something is a little off. His eyebrows are about up to his hairline.

Then I remembered I was nearly naked.

I was like Adam in the Garden of Eden who suddenly feels shame at his nakedness.

I didn't have time to explain.

"Dick, I need some pants. Have you got any in your cruiser you could spare?"

Dick patted down the suspect, put him in handcuffs and slid him into the back of his cruiser. Then he led me over to the trunk and opened it.

He had a lot of gear in there and right on top was a nicely folded pair of jeans. He picked them up and handed them to me.

"Oh this is great. Just great. Thanks so much, Dick," I say, jumping into them as fast as I can and zipping the fly.

"Uh, hey, you wouldn't happen to have any extra shoes or boots with you in here too, would you? I'm sorry to bother you, but...."

Dick shakes his head.

"Sorry, Parker, I don't," he says. "The rest of this stuff is all gear."

"Okay, well then, I am all set with the pants," I say and nod and smile. "They help a lot. Really, thanks so much," I say again and sigh.

I feel a lot better.

Dick is still staring at me like I'm nuts.
I don't know if he's at a loss for words or just
being polite. I'm like a bloodhound on a track.
I can't take the time to explain.

I'm eager to get back into the woods and catch
another runner.

"There were three of them," I tell Dick. "I'm
going back in after another one. I'll be right
back."

Dick nods and a grin comes on his face. He
says, "Okay. I'll be here."

I head off into the woods again barefoot and
shirtless, but feeling a whole lot more like myself
to at least be wearing jeans.

I use the same technique as before, making a
lot of noise and shining my light, then stopping
suddenly, turning the light off and waiting for a
spooked suspect to run.

It takes a little longer as this fellow has made
it farther into the woods. But after a half mile,
I top a rise and from that hill I can hear all
around me.

It isn't long before I hear branches breaking
again. I run towards the sound.

This fellow tries to get away by heading into

a marsh. All it does is bring a swarm of mosquitos our way.

I catch him in the flashlight beam before he gets in deep and tell him to freeze. He keeps running, but just like his buddy, he's about out of gas.

I still don't know which of these guys has a pistol, but if it's him, I could get killed here. I can't risk a guy turning on me at the last second and pulling a trigger.

While he's running, I tackle him from behind too. I tell him he's under arrest, get him to his feet and frisk him.

He doesn't have a weapon. I say, "Start walking," and shine the light in front of him for us both to follow.

This guy walks faster. Maybe the mosquitos get some credit there.

We crest the hill and the blue lights on Trooper Phippen's cruiser guide me back to the scene once again.

He and I appear to still be the only lawmen here. I turn this guy over to Dick too.

Dick cuffs him, searches him, puts him next to the other guy in the back seat of his cruiser and then gives me an update.

"Parker, there's a bunch of wardens on their way to assist," he says.

"Well, there's only one guy left to catch and I can get him," I say. "I can do it."

"That's not the half of it," Dick says. "There's a TV crew headed here with a woman reporter too."

I'm shocked. "What's that about?" I ask Dick.

Dick shrugs and looks all innocent. Then, he says, "I guess they want to see you in your BVDs," and smiles.

"Well, how would they know about that?" I ask Dick, with a knowing look.

He manages to keep a poker face.

Just then the radio crackles to life inside his cruiser, giving him an excuse to not answer me. He bends down, reaches inside the cab and answers the call.

While he's chatting, I'm thinking. And when Dick pops his head back up, I tell him, "I'm leaving. There's no way I am going to be here when the press arrives."

"Get these guys to jail for me, will you, please? I will follow up in the morning. I'm outta here."

The adrenalin was wearing off and my feet were starting to throb something awful.

"Oh!" I add before I leave. "I gotta think that third suspect is still headed for Route 3. He'll be trying to hitch a ride. Come sunup he should be easy to find."

Dick nods.

I shine my light down at my feet. They're scraped raw and swollen. I don't even dare look at my soles.

I limp towards my cruiser like I'm walking barefoot on Popham Beach and a hurricane has littered the shore with broken seashells.

I shine my light at my cruiser. There was air in all four tires and the rear panel was dented but not so badly the tire would rub on the fender. The passenger door was caved in so I'd need a big can opener to get inside. But all I needed was the driver's door.

I slid behind the wheel, fired up the engine, twisted and turned the steering wheel until my grill was pointed towards home, waved to Dick and scooted off into the dark back down the trail as fast as I could.

It seemed to me the cruiser didn't quite track the road like it did before the wrecker broadsided me. But I didn't care.

I was happy just to be escaping the press.

I got back to the house an hour or so before daylight. Rita and Brian were asleep and so was the puppy.

I tiptoed to the bathroom, filled the tub with steaming hot water and slid into it like a man seeking a cure at a sulfur spring. I closed my eyes and dozed off until dawn.

I called into the office later that morning. I learned the third suspect had been collared by Wardens John Blagdon and Lowell Thomas while trying to flag down a ride out of town.

The trio sat in jail while Maine law enforcement began to sort it all out.

We learned one fellow had been released from an Ohio penitentiary just a few weeks earlier. He had a rap sheet about as long as a baboon's arm—a career criminal. I figured he was likely the guy who had shot at me as he had the most to lose.

The other two were local fellows.

One of them finally came clean and told our investigator they'd thrown a party and after drinking all day, they decided they wanted some meat for the grill. They didn't have much money, so they opted for fresh venison.

They learned the hard way it would been a
lot cheaper for them to have gone to a fine
restaurant and dined on prime rib.

The Maine guys were charged not just with the
deer jacking, but eluding an officer and more.

They spent more than a week in jail, paid fines
of $1,000 each and lost their hunting and
fishing privileges too.

Their pal was escorted back to the Ohio
penitentiary and is probably still behind bars.

Dick and I both had our cruisers yanked out of
service. The tote road was not kind to our cars.

My feet took a beating as well. I spent my
evenings soaking them in a hot bath laced
with Epsom Salt. It took more than a week for
them to heal.

It was also kind of tough to walk into the office
on Monday.

Word traveled fast about the Maine warden who
collared some criminals in his underwear.

There were requests for interviews from
reporters all over Maine, and eventually, even
the country.

I wanted to crawl into a cave until all the hoopla

blew over. But I just kept doing my job, while ducking reporters' requests for interviews.

Of course, your colleagues may stop giggling when you walk by after a couple weeks, but this is the kind of career defining episode some never forget.

At my retirement party many years later, friends presented me with a pair of bright white briefs with a Maine warden patch stitched neatly on the front.

They told me they searched, but no one makes trophies for this kinda thing.

"I unzipped my coveralls to my waist, stuck out my chest and shouted, "Hold it right there! Maine game warden! You are all under arrest!"

Spy

I t was the last day of deer rifle season—when some hunters get desperate—and I was out riding in an unmarked cruiser with my brother, Lloyd, alongside me.

He wasn't exactly a deputy warden, but two heads on a swivel are better than one when you're looking for suspicious behavior.

We were looking for signs of illegal hunting when I spied two shiny 4WD vehicles with Rhode Island plates turn off the pavement and go bouncing into the scrub.

I knew that tote road. It was a little used trail to a popular summer camp for kids. It would have been shuttered since late August. Not even a caretaker there now.

These guys had to be headed in there to hunt deer. They hadn't given me any reason to follow them, so I just kept on rolling down the highway. But less than a mile further down the road, I see two more late model SUVs with Rhode Island tags.

These two are parked on the side of the road
with no sign of anyone around. I turn to Lloyd
and grin like I'd just won a prize at the carnival.

"Bingo!" I say and slap the dash for emphasis.
"Brother, we just hit pay dirt!" Lloyd looks at me
like I'm nuts. All he had seen were some cars and
trucks on this road—no deer, not a single hunter.

"I'm pretty sure I know the guys driving those
SUVs and I gotta think they are up to no good,"
I explain to him.

I didn't stop the car or even hit the brakes. Just
in case one of the drivers or passengers was
watching the road from the woods, I didn't want
to give any indication I had any interest in them.

I was able to memorize one of the license plates as
we rolled past. As soon as I was out of sight, I called
into Dispatch and asked them to run the number.

Another half mile down the road, when I felt
confident no one would connect my pulling over
the cruiser with the SUVs, I turned onto the
road shoulder, threw the vehicle into park and
sat waiting for a response from the Dispatcher.

When the radio crackled to life, I felt my hunch
turn into certainty. I learned the plate was
registered to a guy I had busted for illegal
possession of a dead deer a few years earlier.
He had contested the charges and demanded a

trial. The jury hadn't bought his story. He paid a $1,000 fine and spent three nights in jail.

With two SUVs at the camp and another pair a mile down the road, it seemed to me this guy and his buddies were likely organizing a deer drive.

To those that don't know the term, a deer drive is where a line of men spaced maybe 100 feet or more apart walk through the woods and make noise to spook deer from their hiding places toward a line of sharp shooters up ahead. The shooters stand beside trees or sit quietly on ridges or may even get up in tree stands.

Driving deer was legal in Maine when I was a kid. I participated in drives with my family in Jay and Poland growing up. I knew just how it was done.

Deer don't herd up. They bolt when startled. There's a saying among guys who might call themselves hunters, but who are reckless with their rifles. They like to say, "If it's brown, it's down."

When trigger happy shooters pull the trigger on what they think are deer racing through the brush towards them, the results are often tragic. Hunters mistaken for deer are often shot.

So, a lone hunter who wanders unwittingly into the middle of a deer drive is in real danger. I needed a plan—and fast—to catch these guys.

I turned to my brother and said, "It will be dusk in a little more than two hours. These guys must be desperate to get a deer. They're going to be driving and I'm going to catch them."

"By yourself?" Lloyd says, incredulous. "But you've got no idea how many guys are even out there. There could be a dozen or more. How are you going to do this by yourself?"

"I've got an idea," I say confidently. "I haven't got time to explain it though. You just get behind the wheel and drive outta here. Drive anywhere you want—just not along this road. Stay at least two miles from here."

Lloyd nods and listens hard. "After dark, drive the cruiser over to the house and just wait for me to call you," I tell him.

"Okay, I'll do it," Lloyd says. "But be careful, Parker. This is really dangerous, you know."

"I know, I know," I say with a scowl. "But I'll be okay. You slide on over here behind the wheel. Just don't take off until I get some stuff out of the trunk first."

"I got it," Lloyd says. "But I mean it. Be careful. I'll be at your house waiting for you to call me to come get you."

I poke my head out of the driver's side window.

No one's coming in either direction. I jump out
of the cruiser, pop the trunk and get into my
disguise as fast as I can.

I'm in my uniform and I need to hide it.
I shimmy into dark blue coveralls and zip it up
high to just under my chin. Then I add a blaze
orange vest over that and don a frayed, blaze
orange cap to top it off.

I grab my rifle from the back seat, shut the
trunk, give it a good double bump to signal
Lloyd I'm done and he roars off.

I look up and down the road one more time to
make certain no one is watching me and I race
across the road and into the woods. I'd run less
than 200 feet when I hear two shots maybe 500
yards in front of me off to my left.

I reach through the slit pocket in my overalls, into
a pocket on my uniform and pull out my compass.
I get a bearing on where the shots came from,
look up and plot a path. These guys are on the
move. It won't do me any good to head for where
they were. I have to get in front of them and let
them run into me.

My plan is to intercept the first driver and work
my way down their line, then make a loop around
and up to the line of shooters and say hello. I'm
running a big horseshoe in hopes of locating
and identifying all the guys involved here.

I had to hustle to catch up with them but also be careful not to appear to be in a hurry when I did find them. That might give me away too.

I ran through the woods for five minutes until I caught sight of a hunter in front of me. I slowed to a walk and approached. It was a big guy wearing a blaze orange hat and carrying an expensive Belgian shotgun.

I startled him.

I introduced myself saying, "I live on the farm just down the road. My brother and I are out hunting. We split up but I said we'd meet up at the camp up ahead at dusk."

"Oh," the guy said. I could see his shoulders relax. "Yeah, we're all meeting up there later too." I smile and nod.

"Say, I heard a shot a few minutes ago, was that you?" I ask him.

"No, it was my cousin off to my left," he said. "He musta seen a deer."

"Oh," I say. "Well, I gotta keep going," and I start to walk off.

"Hey, be careful walking through here," the big hunter warns me. "There are three more guys walking right up through here."

He's stopping just short of telling me he and his buddies are driving deer.

"Thanks, I will," I say. And as soon as I am out of his sight, I throw the rifle sling over my left shoulder, reach through the slit in my coveralls for the pencil and paper in my uniform, and scribble notes about this guy while walking.

I note what he's wearing, along with his approximate age, height, weight, eye color, note a mole on his cheek, crooked lower teeth and more.

Then, I tuck the paper into my pocket and keep moving until I run into the next fellow, who is also carrying a shotgun. I introduce myself and tell him the same story. I ask him if he had fired his gun and he says, "Yeah, that was me. Don't know if I got him though."

Looking down at his shotgun, I said, "You hunting rabbits?"

"Nah," he says, making a face like he'd just poured some spoiled half and half into his coffee. "We don't hunt no rabbits. We's deah huntin'."

"Well, how come you're carrying a shotgun then?" I ask him.

"Shotguns is safer," he says like he's explaining ballistics to a 10 year old boy. "The bullets don't go so far."

He pauses and looks down at my rifle, then back up at my face. I get the feeling he thinks maybe I'm the village idiot and I shouldn't be out here by myself.

"Oh, right," I say and nod in agreement.

As he answers my questions, I'm again making a long list of mental notes about his appearance. This fellow was shorter, heavier, older. He had salt and pepper hair, a cleft chin, a gold capped incisor and a double chin.

"I gotta get going," he said. "Be careful walkin' through here. My two buddies are huntin' nearby. You don't wanna get yoself shot."

My eyes opened wide and I nodded big—like I figured the idiot he believed me to be would do.

"I sure don't!" I said, "Thanks!" and I marched off.

Two more guys to go. I managed to run into both of them, repeated my story about meeting up with my brother at dark and as soon as I was out of sight of each one, I again grabbed by pencil and pad and scribbled notes to remind me where they were in the sequence and their distinctive features.

A deer drive often has an equal number of guys driving at one end and shooting—or planning to shoot—on the other end.

So, once I got through the four guys, I guess I'm after eight of them.

I look at the sky and my watch. Both tell me there's not a lot of daylight left. I run around the edge of the drivers, pausing to stop and listen and look now and again.

I'm looking for a shooter partially hidden by a tree trunk, atop a ridge, or with his back braced against a big rock. Maine's mandatory orange law helps.

I spy a guy in a blaze orange cap standing beside a big pine maybe 100 yards from the camp.

I pretend to run into him by accident. He sees me and hisses, "Hey! Buddy! Whacha doin'? You tryin' to get yohself killed or somethin'?"

I look around like maybe he's talking to someone else and he motions me closer to him.

I tell him the same "just looking for my brother" tale.

He shakes his head at me like I'm walking through a minefield.

"You gotta be careful! There's guys huntin' all around you out here. You could get hurt bad!" he says.

"Really?" I say feigning shock. I open my eyes

wide and my mouth to match. "How many guys do you think are out here?"

"I got three buddies right through those trees," he says nodding and looking in a straight line over a ridge.

"Gosh," I say. "Well, I will be extra careful then. Thanks a lot."

And I walk the way he directed me, found his pals and repeated the farm boy story again and again and again.

I had notes on every one of them now. I had a facial description, their position in this illegal hunt, what each was wearing and what brand of shotgun each was carrying. I just had to spring the trap.

I hustle around the far edge of the group and run through the woods until I can circle back to the kids' camp.

Two big red SUVs are parked side by side waiting for my suspects. I look around for a place to wait for them to arrive. I settle on the porch of the camp store about 30 feet from their vehicles. I sit down on the steps, with my rifle across my lap and wait for the hunters to come out of the brush.

It was close to dark. I'd need a flashlight soon.

Each of them saw me when they walked out
of the woods. But none of them thought my
presence was odd, because I had told each of
them I would be meeting my brother here.

They were chatting amiably with one another
and saying things like, "Hey, so it wasn't our
day. We'll get 'em next year," and things like
that. Despite the cheating, they were going
home without any deer.

I sat on the steps and pretended to be looking
around for my brother while keeping one eye on
the crew.

They popped the hatches on the SUVs and one
by one unloaded their shotguns and then laid
their weapons down in the back.

Two or three removed their hunting coats so
they would be more comfortable on the ride
home. They were talking about how good dinner
was going to taste as they began to climb into
the two SUVs, preparing to drive away.

Eight guys, two vehicles, one of me.

I stood up and leaned my rifle against the porch
post, unzipped my coveralls to my waist, stuck
out my chest and shouted, "Hold it right there!
Maine game warden! You are all under arrest!"

Guys who were just about to lower their large

fannies onto the cushions of the SUVs stopped in mid drop. No one said a word.

It was a kind of Superman moment and just like in the comic books, the bad guys froze. They were stunned.

I picked up my rifle and walked quickly towards them, a man in command.

"I want all your licenses on the hood of this vehicle," I said pointing to the SUV closest to me. A couple of the guys looked at one another and shrugged. I knew I had to get their attention or I risked losing control of the situation.

I ran up into the face of the biggest guy and shouted, "NOW!" like a crazed drill sergeant with fresh recruits.

The mood changed immediately. Some of them began digging through their hunting clothes for their wallets. Others held their hands up and said, "Okay, Okay. Relax!"

Just because I had seen all of these men empty their shotguns and lay them in the back of both SUVs, didn't mean they were unarmed.

Once I had all their licenses on the hood, I instructed them all to step back and put their arms up in the air while I checked each of them for concealed weapons.

Sure enough, three of the fellows were carrying some heavy duty caliber handguns under their coats. They weren't the type of sidearms used by Maine hunters.

With those out of their possession, I got down to the business of studying their hunting licenses.

Maine employed a punch system at the time. If you had killed and reported a deer, your license got a hole punched in it.

I was stunned to see that seven of the eight hunters' licenses had already been punched. Only one of these guys had not legally taken a deer this year.

That meant seven of them had no right to be hunting deer today, let alone participate in an illegal deer drive.

And looking at the names on the licenses, I realized three of the fellows were guys I had arrested a few years earlier. This trio was facing some significant time in jail if convicted. I saw the look on their faces. They knew they were in big trouble.

But how was I going to get all these guys to the jail in Waterville? Lloyd had my cruiser. I didn't have a radio with me. Dick Tracy cartoons might have that private investigator sporting a wrist phone, but the invention of cell phones was decades away.

I bluffed.

I said, "Okay, fellows. We've got a couple choices here. I can call this in on my portable radio and a bunch of cruisers will show up to take you to jail for processing. Of course, it could take a couple hours for them to get here, depending on what else they have going on. And your vehicles will have to be towed."

There were scowls.

"Or," I continued, "I can ride with four of you in one vehicle and the other four of you can follow and drive yourselves to jail. That will be a lot faster. And this way, your cars won't be towed either. But it's up to you. You tell me how you want to do this."

It was dark now. Cold too. I could see my breath as I explained the situation.

"We'll drive. We'll drive," one of the fellows said and the others nodded in agreement.

I nod and try not to smile.

"Okay," I say, and I give them the street address. "I will ride in the first vehicle in the back and be watching. Let's go."

We start for jail, and the guys in my car all start complaining.

I shut that down fast to prevent an uprising. "It might not be wise for you guys to be talking about this in front of me. You might want to just be quiet and enjoy the ride."

The looks on their faces made it clear they didn't like my advice, but they took it.

At the Waterville Police Department, all eight guys sullenly climb out of the SUVs and shuffle into the station with me following behind.

The police officer behind the desk looks at me like I'm crazy, bringing in all these hunters.

"How many prisoners do you have?" he asks.

"Eight," I say.

"Where are the other arresting officers?" he asks, craning his neck to look behind me and beyond the pile of prisoners crowding the waiting room.

"There's only me," I say.

He looks more than a little alarmed. "Well, do they have any weapons?" he asks.

It was a good question, especially since they were all dressed to kill—deer, that is.

"There's a load of shotguns in the back of their

SUVs outside," I answer him going down the list. "Some of them were carrying handguns too. I took them and put them with the shotguns."

"They are all probably carrying hunting knives too," I add. "I didn't bother to take those."

Well, the thought these guys might all be carrying knives with blades up to 12 inches long under their coats, makes his eyes pop.

He bends down and pushes a button on some intercom device and barks orders. When that doesn't get a response, he dashes around his desk, into the back room and yells, "I need help NOW!"

A second officer rushes out of the back room. Together the officers ask the hunters to open their coats and remove any and all weapons before being placed in holding cells.

I start filling out paperwork. I am about half way through when one of the older hunters calls me over, glares at me and says, "I want you to know I think you treated us some rotten. If I were you, I would stay out of Rhode Island."

I stand up straight, take a half step forward so our chins are centimeters apart and say, "I'm not going to be intimidated by you or anyone else. I have a job to do and I did it. You guys hunt here all the time. You own property here. We know who you are. All we ask is that you follow the rules, same as everyone else. If not, well, I might just catch you again."

The eight of them went into the holding cells grousing and demanding to call their attorneys. They yelled over to me, saying I would never be able to make the charges stick. They told me I was wasting my time.

I handed my paperwork to the officer in charge, borrowed a phone and called my brother and asked him to come get me.

When Lloyd picked me up and saw the two SUVs out front, he wanted to hear all what happened out there.

Telling him the story as he drove us home helped me cement the details in my mind. I pulled my pencil and paper out and made even more notes on each of the eight guys I'd just put behind bars.

I was happy with myself for collaring these guys, but I was smart enough to know this case was far from over.

"So, they grew moustaches. So, they
brought a bunch of their relatives up
here with them for the trial.
So what? I can identify every one
of the Defendants, I say."

Disguise

N early six months had passed after my deer drive bust, when I got a call from the District Attorney's Office telling me the case was on the court docket for the next week. This was a busy office. They'd appointed an assistant to handle it. He had some questions for me.

Could I stop by the office?

I'd worked with a number of Prosecutors from counties all over the state. I knew the name and I knew this fellow was conscientious.

When I strolled into his office later that same day, he put it plainly. "Their attorneys are throwing the spaghetti at this one, Warden," he said.

"Spaghetti?" I smiled. "Is that a legal term?"

"I mean they are arguing anything and everything to try and get the charges dropped. And they're spending a bundle of money on legal power to do it too," he chuckled.

"How many lawyers are we talking about here?"

I ask. "Three top attorneys from three top law firms. One from Rhode Island, two from right here in Maine," he says.

I shake my head and chuckle. Maybe some of these guys have a criminal record elsewhere, and if convicted in Maine, it could hurt them in their home state. You just never know.

"Don't worry. I got 'em dead to rights," I tell the Prosecutor. "They know it and I know it."

He purses his lips and shakes his head as if he isn't convinced. Then he picks up an inch thick stack of papers and starts thumbing through it and paraphrasing what he's reading.

"Eight guys, one warden, late in the day, you arresting all of them when it was dark, no dead deer. It says you didn't even see any of the Defendants actually shoot at anything."

"I heard two shots," I said. "One of them admitted to shooting at a deer."

He sets the stack down, looks me hard in the eye and says, "The Defense is arguing these guys were all just gathering together at the end of the day for the ride home and you got it wrong."

I was just about to respond when he sighs and adds, "Actually, they are arguing just about everything in the book. But I think their argument about just getting together at the end of the day might be enough to persuade a judge they're innocent."

"No, I got them dead to rights," I tell him. "It was clear from the pattern they were walking, how they warned me about their friends down the line, where their vehicles were left. They were driving deer."

"This is just the tip of the iceberg," the Prosecutor tells me, running his hands through his thinning hair. "Once we get inside the courtroom, you can be certain they will do even more to create doubt in the judge's mind."

He sits down on the edge of his desk, looks me hard in the eye and says, "I'm telling you, I have some serious concerns here. I'm not sure a judge is going to buy your bust."

"It will be fine," I say, trying to allay his fears. "You just put me on the stand and I will explain exactly what I saw and what happened. It's an open and shut deer driving case."

The Prosecutor shakes his head and smiles at me like I live in the Land of Simple People. His look reminded me of the way those Rhode Island guys had looked at me in the woods when I told them I was going to meet my brother.

"I'm telling you the Defense is treating this deer driving case like it was Murder One," he says, his voice rising in exasperation. "They are pulling out all the stops."

He reaches behind him and picks up a folder four inches thick and then lets it plop back down on his desk, then jams his right index finger into it like he wished it was a magic wand and he could make this whole case just disappear.

"This file is just for one of your Defendants," he tells me. "They are trying to drown the office in paperwork too." He stands up and stretches his back, walks to a window and looks down at the street below.

"Just tell me what it is you are so worried about," I push him.

"Well, first of all, we are talking eight Defendants," he says, turning to look at me. "How are you going to be able to identify each of them? It was dark when they came out of the woods.

They were all wearing hats and hunting pants and jackets. They will be wearing suits at the trial. You put the wrong face to the wrong name on just one of these guys, or hesitate in any way, and the judge will toss the whole case out. You have to be 100 percent—dead on—with your testimony—not one single error. Nothing at all."

"I can ID every one of them," I say confidently.
He stares into my eyes. "I don't know," he says,

again. "I've got real doubts about your testimony being so ironclad we can beat their high priced legal team. We are talking lawyers who've successfully defended some of the most notorious cases in New England."

He sighs, walks back to his chair and tosses a pencil on his desk in frustration.

"And also, I have to say, my office has a huge caseload, as you know. So, to be devoting so much of my time to a deer driving case... Well, I'm not sure it's the best use of Maine taxpayers' dollars."

"I will identify every one of those guys," I say again and stand up to leave.

"I sure hope so," he sighs and stands up to see me to the door. "The trial is set for Monday at 10 a.m. Be at the courthouse at 9 a.m. sharp, please. We'll know more then."

"I'll be there," I tell him.

Over the weekend, I went over the facts and reviewed my sworn affidavit. I didn't see any holes. It all looked solid.

But pulling up to the courthouse on Monday, I saw the lengths the Defendants were willing to go to wriggle out of a conviction.

There were three fellows in Italian suits and shoes

polished so bright you could use them to signal for help if you were lost in the woods. Each held a monogrammed briefcase. I wasn't quite sure why they were waiting on the courthouse steps instead of going inside.

I heard a little murmur go through the crowd and looked up and saw why these guys were there.

Rolling slowly up the street to the courthouse steps was a string of six white stretch limousines.

I stood there watching as, one by one, an impeccably dressed driver got out of each limo, put a black cap squarely on his head, then walked to the back door and opened it wide.

From each vehicle, stepped six guys in matching suits and sunglasses sporting moustaches. They stood tall, smiled confidently and walked up the steps and into the courthouse, with not so much as a hello to the fancy fellows with the briefcases.

I could see what they were doing. And it was pretty clever.

The eight Defendants had brought up another couple dozen family members—all with similar features. They'd worked to change their hair and they'd grown moustaches too. It was all an attempt to make it impossible for me to identify the eight hunters from last November.

These fellows standing outside were their
legal team. They had instructed all of the
Defendants not to so much as smile or nod
at their attorneys. That was clever too. If I
witnessed any sign, any conversation, it might
help me to identify them.

Smart. Really smart.

I stepped inside and was met by the Prosecutor.
I could tell he was nervous and working hard to
keep his composure.

He smiled and escorted me into an anteroom
off the trial chamber and shut the door. Once
inside, his whole demeanor changed from
confident to panic.

"Look, if there are any of these guys you are
going to have trouble identifying, I need to know
right now, before we get before the judge.
I mean, this is it. I gotta know where we stand."

"I told you. It won't be a problem," I said.

"Have you seen these guys? All of them? There
must be like 35 guys inside the courtroom now
and they all look alike!" he says with his voice
rising. "How are you going to know who is who?"

He reminds me of an exasperated parent talking
to a four year old before the whole family piles
into the car and heads out on a long trip. You

know the line, "Have you gone to the bathroom?"
"I can identify all of them," I say again.

"Well, you had better go in there and take a look
around!" he tells me—like Mom warning me
again to run back into the house for another try.

I said again, "No need to. I can do this. I will
get all of them."

In retrospect, maybe I should have done what he
asked. It would have made him feel better. But I
didn't.

The Prosecutor looked hard at me again, sighed,
looked at his watch and said, "Twenty minutes
until trial. I'm going across the hall and talk to
the Defense. Just wait here."

He picked up a file, opened the door and walked the
eight feet across the aisle to greet the Defense team
with a big fake smile plastered across his face.

I stood there alone, a witness to four guys in
expensive suits and haircuts all smiling and shaking
hands like they were preparing for an afternoon of
golf with the President of the United States.

The whole bunch of them went into a room
across the hall and shut the door.

Ten minutes later, the Prosecutor comes out
of the room smiling and I see him shaking

hands again with the each of the three Defense Attorneys. It's like they are all members of some secret lodge. It makes the hair on the back of my neck stand up.

My guy opens the door, and with the look of a fellow who just got a great deal on a new car, says, "I offered them a plea deal and they took it."

"You did WHAT?" I say in disbelief, rising from my chair.

He says again, "I offered to let them plead it down and they took it," and while his smile is fading at my reaction, it's clear he sees this as a victory.

I feel my blood pressure spiking.

"Are you serious? Whatever happened to discussing a plea deal with the arresting officer first?" I admonished him. I'm getting a little loud.

He stands up straight, looks over his shoulder to make sure no one has heard me outside in the hall, and scowls at me.

"I'm sorry. But I couldn't take the chance you wouldn't be able to identify all eight of these guys." His voice is part hiss, part whisper.

He leans in closer and says, "If you can't identify every single one of them—in the order you met them—we'd lose everything. No case."

He stands up straight and takes a big breath and throws his shoulders back. "At least this way, the State gets something."

I'm flabbergasted.

"I'm really disappointed in you," I say. "Maybe you shouldn't have this job."

He's offended at my remark. "That was uncalled for," he tells me. "I have put a lot of hours into this case."

I'm shaking my head in disbelief. I was an hour away from a conviction on a big case and it has all gone up in smoke because he doesn't believe in me.

The Prosecutor sees I'm upset and adds, "I'm sorry. But I think I did the best I could here given the circumstances."

"Circumstances? What circumstances?" I say, shaking my head in disbelief.

"So, they grew moustaches. So, they brought a bunch of their relatives up here with them for the trial. So what? I've told you over and over, I can identify every one of the Defendants," I tell him again.

"No," the attorney says. "I don't think you can." He might as well have just told me he thinks I'm delusional. "I honestly don't know anybody who could pick the correct eight Defendants from that courtroom crowd."

I turn towards him and say, "Well, how about I go into that courtroom right now and do it? Hunh? Would you believe me then?"

"You still believe you can do it?" he says to me. He's looking deep into my eyes like I'm an unique combination of crazy and stubborn. "You really want to go in there and try?"

"Absolutely," I tell him. "But when I identify all of them, it's not going to make you look very smart, because you just cut them all a deal."

His chin shoots up like I have just grazed him with a sharp right hook. He gets a crooked smile on his face and a steely glint in his eyes. He doesn't like me challenging him. He stands up tall and takes a deep breath.

"I have to go into the courtroom with the Defense and put this plea agreement into the record, before the judge," he says, thinking out loud. "But after that, if the other parties agree, well, there's nothing scheduled for the rest of the day. We expected this trial to take all day."

He's rubbing his chin and thinking he might as well have a little fun now. When I fall flat on my face, it will prove just how wise he was to plea bargain the case.

"So, okay. Sure. If the other side agrees, I'd love to see you try and identify all eight of them," he tells me. "I'll go ask them right now. Just wait here."

The Prosecutor steps outside of the room.

I stand up and walk back over to the six inch wide by two foot long window in the door—just big enough so people can see if anyone is using the room, I guess. I sidle up next to it, stand back at an angle and watch the action outside.

I see my guy bend in and chat with the Defense. The other attorneys break into big grins, shake their heads and reach into their pockets for their wallets—like they're wanting to place bets.

But they stop short of actually pulling money out of their fat billfolds and making a bet. Watching them in silence, it is clear to me none of them believe I can identify the Defendants.

A woman comes out of the courtroom and shushes the attorneys and lets them know the judge is about to take the bench.

The four lawyers go from boisterous bettors to altar boys in the blink of an eye. They straighten their backs and parade into the chamber as solemn as ushers at a church service.

I shake my head, turn and take my seat at the

table again and wait. A half hour later, the Prosecutor is back. He looks relieved.

"Okay, Warden Tripp," he says rubbing his hands together with glee. "The plea agreement is on the record. This case is over. Now, if you still want to try identifying all the hunters you cited that day, the Defense has said they are fine with letting you try. The blackboard is still set up and the courtroom is all yours. I just want to be clear the judge will not be present and whatever you say will not affect this case at all. It's over. This is purely for show."

He grins big at me, pauses and adds, "And, if you've changed your mind, and you don't want to do it, that's fine too."

"No, I haven't changed my mind," I tell him. "Let's go."

"Okay, follow me," he says and opens the door big for me to walk out in front of him. I feel like a trick dog headed into the circus ring. He's sporting a big smile that tells me he is looking forward to my act.

I enter the chamber and see for the first time, he wasn't kidding when he said these guys had packed the room with their relatives. There are about 40 men in the room and 35 of them look remarkably alike.

It felt like I'd stumbled into a funeral parlor
where the elderly mother of a dozen sons will be
eulogized shortly. Sons, cousins and uncles have
all donned their best suits and solemnly gathered
here for the matriarch's memorial service.

I'm looking at a sea of moustached males. The
eight guys I'd arrested six months earlier are
mixed into this mob.

I walk up to the board, scan all the faces, pick
up a piece of chalk and start talking.

I draw the deer drive—four drivers, four shooters,
make a heading for each. I assign a number to
each of the positions as I had encountered the
hunters in the woods the previous year.

I give a little background on the case. The
road, the time of day, where I had seen the
two SUVs pull into the tote road leading to the
camp and then the second group of hunters a
mile farther down the road.

The attorneys are all good students. They
appear mesmerized by my testimony. The
fellows behind the railing pretend they aren't
much interested.

No one says a word. You can hear a pin drop.

I explain how I approached each one of the men
that day, our conversation, what each hunter was

wearing and then I spelled all their names one by one in the order I ran into them—below the eight Xs.

I look back at the audience and see a few of the smug smiles evaporate. They are surprised I am able to remember all the names in order and spell them correctly.

Some of the guys start to fidget in their seats. Others lean in.

I stop, put the pen down and announce, "Before I go any further, I want to identify the men I arrested three years ago for illegal possession of deer. I see they are here today too. Please, stand up when I point to you and call your name."

Well, that kind of shook them all up. The crowd didn't know if I was just stalling or showing off. For the record, I was doing both.

I point to the fellows from the case years earlier, one by one, name them and they reluctantly stand up and stare at the floor.

From the corner of my eye, I see the Defense Attorneys' mouths fall open. They begin poking each other in the ribs and whispering to one another.

I'm no lip reader, but I get the distinct impression they are saying something like, "Hey, he's doing pretty good here!"

After proving I recognized the scofflaws I'd arrested three years ago, even though two of them had put on weight, lost hair and grown moustaches, I say, "Thank you. You can be seated."

I wasn't nervous, but I wanted all those fellows who had something to hide to squirm a little.

"Now, let me turn to this deer driving case," I say. "I'm going to start with the first hunter on the blackboard here and go on down the list in order, from one to eight. When I point to you and call your name, please, stand up and stay standing until I tell you all to be seated."

I scan the chamber one last time. I want to do this without any hesitation, so there can be no question I'm not like a guy in a blindfold throwing darts at the wall and hoping to get lucky.

There were no identical twins in the audience, but a couple of them weren't far from it.

Some of the fellows stared straight ahead with shark eyes. Others had a kind of tough guy smirk on their faces like they were inconvenienced being asked to pose for a mug shot. A couple of the fellows just looked sour—like they needed antacids or hemorrhoid cream.

I pause for dramatic effect and look across the room, once, twice, three times and finally, with all eyes on me, I take a deep breath and begin:

"Left side of the courtroom. Second row, fourth from the right. You are hunter number one and your name is... Please, stand up," and on down the list I go, giving each man time to stand and react to being correctly identified and for everyone present to realize I had correctly identified the hunters—in the order I had encountered them in the woods.

By the time I get to number six, even some the guys in the crowd were shaking their heads and looking at me like I was some sort of magician. Fact is, I have always had a gift for remembering names and faces.

I identify them all—all eight. And when I'm done, I look over at the Prosecutor. He looks at me, a little dumbfounded. Then he turns left, looking over at the Defense, to see if they agree with me.

The opposing attorneys nod their heads up and down in the affirmative. They grin. One of them even gives my guy two thumbs up.

After a moment of silence, it all sinks in. The Defense table erupts with all three attorneys jumping out of their chairs, laughing and guffawing like they'd bet the farm on a long shot and their horse won by two lengths.

I look over at the Prosecutor. His mouth drops open and his head slowly sinks to his chest. He pretends he's inspecting a stain on his tie.

He realizes he's given the Defense a big win because he doubted me.

I admit, I didn't have a whole lot of sympathy for him right then.

The lead Defense Attorney struts over to the Prosecutor, sticks his hand out, laughs and says, "Well, Sir, your witness did it. I wouldn't have thought in a million years he could have identified every single one of my clients, in order, but he did."

"Of course," he was quick to add, "I don't want you to, in any way, misconstrue my praise for Warden Tripp's gifts of recall as the slightest admission of my clients' actual guilt. My clients were wrongly accused and our duly recorded settlement stands. But, I must say, that was an impressive display of facial recognition and recall. Truly. Very impressive, indeed."

The Defendants' lead counsel turns and faces me. He raises his right arm and pinches his thumb and index finger together, as if he is tipping his hat to me and smiles.

Then he turns back to the Prosecutor and grins like the proverbial cat who has just swallowed the canary.

The other two members of his legal team join him and all three of them pound the Prosecutor

on the back and shake his hand repeatedly.
It was like he had just scored the winning
touchdown for their team.

And, in essence, he had. This plea bargain he
gave them was a big win for their team. The
eight hunters paid a collective fine of just a few
thousand dollars. None of them got any jail time.

I walked out of the courthouse a few minutes
later with my chin up, but pretty unhappy about
how this particular case turned out.

I consoled myself on the drive home,
knowing word would spread fast about how
I had managed to pick these guys out of the
crowd—and the three others from the earlier
case—despite their clever disguises.

I figured they'd all think twice about staging
another deer drive in my district. And if they
did cheat again, I was confident I'd get more help
from the District Attorney's Office next time.

I'd studied the Prosecutor's face as those big city
lawyers laughed and slapped him on the back.
I'd also read his mind. It said:

No more plea bargains for you.

*"The woman who has beaten me bloody
with the fly rod is headed my way
carrying a pickaxe."*

Fireworks

On July 4th, 1976, when thousands of Maine residents were happily celebrating our nation's bicentennial, my partner, Greg Maher, and I came close to getting killed.

We were patrolling Big Lake by boat. We knew we would find a lot of people fishing, driving their boats and enjoying the water. We were checking fishing licenses and making certain people were safe.

There was nothing fancy about our ride that day. It was a 14 foot, deep V aluminum hull with a tiller driven 20 horse power outboard motor. There was no state seal on the side. We were in uniform, but we weren't wearing our wide brimmed hats—the wind would blow them off.

Greg was in the stern, steering the boat. I was sitting in the bow.

We approached Peter Dana Point and noticed a newly built pier with a sturdy floating raft at the end. An adult male was fishing off the dock and there were two little kids, maybe five or six years old, beside him, holding rods too.

Greg idled the engine and we each lifted our binoculars to take a closer look at the man's activities.

We were far enough back so they wouldn't be likely to look up and see us.

After a minute or so of watching, Greg suggested we go on over and check the fellow out. The little kids didn't need a license to fish. I nodded and off we went, with Greg expertly pulling alongside their floating dock a minute or so later.

As we approached, adults on shore raised their heads to watch our progress.

A woman with long hair and another man walked onto the dock and joined the threesome on the raft.

I stepped out of the bow and tied the bowline on a cleat. Greg shut off the motor, then climbed out and secured the stern with his line.

We introduced ourselves to the fellow fishing and Greg asked to see his fishing license.

The woman who had walked out to meet us crossed her arms across her chest and said defiantly, "He's just visiting. He doesn't need a license. He's an Indian. Indians don't need licenses."

It was clear from her tone she greatly resented our presence.

And she was close to right about the fellow not needing a fishing license issued by the state of Maine if he was the member of a recognized tribe. Except the law was a little more complicated than that at the time, as many are.

An Indian first needed to get on the Tribal Council list. If they were on that list, then a Maine fishing license was free to them. But they still had to have a Maine license.

Greg asked the fellow for his fishing license. "I don't have one," he said.

So Greg asked to see his driver's license and the fellow reaches into his back pocket for his wallet, opens it up, finds his driver's license and hands it to Greg. He was cooperating but the woman is scowling at us big time.

The two little kids hang on the woman's skirt and peek out at us.

I'm looking around the dock admiring the new construction as all this is going on. I see the head of a nail sticking up about two inches, right in the path of these kids—who are barefoot.

I don't want to see them, or anyone, get hurt.
They could rip their feet up bad on that nail head.

I look at them and nod and point to the nail.
"See that?" I ask them. I don't expect an
answer. "Dangerous. Needs a hammer," and
as they are little ones, I make a motion with my
right hand twice—as if I am pounding a nail.

The kids eyes open wide when our eyes meet.
They turn and look at each other and then dash
away up the dock, into the house.

I turn my attention back to Greg. He looks at the
man's driver's license and hands it back to him.

"I'm just going to give you a warning," he says.
"This isn't a citation. There's no fine or court
date. But I need for you to get a license. Okay?"
Greg says.

Greg is doing the guy a favor. He could have
cited him.

The guy nods like he understands. But he
doesn't smile or show any emotion.

Greg takes his pen from his breast pocket and
then his summons book and begins to fill out
the paperwork.

The silence gives me a moment to point out the
nail head to the fisherman. He walks a half

dozen steps over to a tool box, flips open the lid, comes back with a hammer and pounds the nail flush with the board in two whacks.

I smile, thinking I've done a good thing. A few seconds later, Greg is done writing. He hands the fellow his warning and his driver's license, then slides his summons book and pen back into his breast pocket.

Greg and I are just about to smile and say, "Thanks a lot and have a nice holiday weekend," and step back into our boat, when we hear a booming male voice shouting from shore.

We look up the dock.

Bearing down on us like a Spanish fighting bull is a very large fellow, bellering, "Get off my dock!"

The fisherman and the woman step aside as he comes pounding towards us. The raft rocks beneath our feet.

I expect the guy to stop and talk to us.

Instead, he lowers his head and plows it into my chest like he's sacking a quarterback.

I am knocked clean off the dock and fly through the air. I land in the bottom of our boat in a heap—my head slams the transom.

I see flashes of light. But I shake my head and sit up immediately and look for Greg.

I see the big man grab the hammer off the dock, cock it back over his head like a tomahawk and lunge at Greg.

It's clear this guy intends to kill him.

Greg ducks his head and throws his arms up —locking one hand around his other wrist—to block the hammer blow.

I get to my feet, scramble out of the boat and onto the dock and jump onto the back of the giant attacking Greg.

If the guy was smaller, I could have gotten my arms around his chest. But he's huge.

Greg is in front. He grabs the big man's forearms and the two of them are grunting, spinning and pushing each other around the dock like Russian wrestlers.

Trouble is, this isn't a fair match at all. The fellow attacking Greg outweighs him by more than 50 pounds and he's a foot taller.

The big man isn't too impressed by me on his back either. He won't let go of the hammer. He is twisting and tugging, trying to break Greg's grip so he can take another swing at Greg's head.

I drop back down to the dock, looking for a chance to leap up and steal the hammer from the giant's hand.

Greg and the bruiser spin around the dock, grimacing and locked in combat. The dock is rocking violently beneath our feet.

I see a chance to take the weapon away. I leap, miss and get a sharp elbow poked into my left eye on the way down. I squint, bend at the knees and wait for another opening.

Greg and the man circle dangerously close to the dock's edge.

Suddenly, the big guy stumbles and he and Greg tumble into the lake, arms still locked together, glaring at one another.

I dash, get down on my knees, and lean over, my arms at the ready to help Greg.

When the two men surface, they gasp and sputter. I see the hammer is gone from the big fellow's hand. He's down to bare fists.

Greg has managed to get his flashlight out of his belt holder. He's holding it up behind his head, ready to strike.

I'm concerned the big man may be able to wrestle the light away from Greg and use it against him.

I bend down and shout in Greg's ear, "Just push him over to me and I will put the cuffs on him." I figure that's a lot safer. Greg nods.

I reach over and yank the flashlight out of Greg's hand so he will have more control.

I place it on the dock, but the raft is rocking. It rolls into the lake. I grab my handcuffs from my belt.

Greg has managed to push the big man against the pier, within my reach.

I'm reaching out to grab ahold of the attacker's right wrist when I feel the back of my skull slammed with what feels like a rock.

I throw my left arm up and duck underneath my elbow to see what is going on.

The woman who had challenged us earlier is swinging a fly rod at me as hard and fast as she can. She's got the tip of the rod in both hands and is beating me with the reel and handle.

I'm here to tell you, the edges on fly rod reels are a lot sharper than they look—or they are when they are smacking you in the skull at 60 miles an hour anyway.

I turn back to help Greg.

She gets four or five good whacks into me

because I can't take time to stop her. I may get hurt, but Greg could be killed.

I strain, trying to get ahold of the man's wrist.

I feel something running into my eyes and blink a few times, thinking it's lake water. It's making it hard for me to see.

I taste blood and realize the woman who has smashed me in the head has opened up my scalp.

Greg and the fellow continue to exchange blows and are flipping and flopping every which way. The water and blood makes it hard for me to see. And this big man pulls away every time I get close with the cuffs.

I keep at it for what seems like minutes, but it was probably only seconds.

I feel another three hard whacks across my skull. I cringe and duck my head.

I'm hit again, a fourth time, and it hurts a little less. I see something dark—the size of a hockey puck—go flying off into the lake.

It's the reel. She's beat me so hard with it, my skull has busted it in two. It pays to be hard headed.

I keep straining to reach the wet wrist of the giant.

I clamp my right hand onto the guy's wrist and prepare to cuff him with my left, when I feel the back of my shirt pulled up between my shoulder blades.

It's the quiet fellow Greg had written the warning to. He's been inspired to join the fray.

He bends down low over my back, his arms tugging on my soaked shirt. He's trying his best to pull away from the big man in the water, who is now attempting to drown Greg like a giant raccoon on a young hound.

I grit my teeth and throw my upper body forward. The guy bends lower. I feel his hot breath on my neck.

I have no choice. I let go of the big man's wrist, make a fist and snap my elbow up and back as hard and fast as I can. My knuckles catch the New Yorker square in the nose.

I hear an "Unh!" and big feet stumbling backwards. He falls in a heap behind me somewhere.

Free from attack, I finally manage to get one cuff on the guy in the water.

Of course, the fellow is furious. And that creates another problem. He's like a swordfish fighting for his life. He explodes out of the water, yanks his arms away and throws more wild roundhouse punches at both me and Greg.

My face is slapped silly with the loose end of the cuffs. Greg duck his head back, but gets clipped by the cuffs.

It's hard to see the handcuffs because they are silver and in the churned up water, the color blends into the glare of the July sun and white water. But I sure feel the steel bracelet when it smacks me in the face.

I feel the dock rock behind me and know someone is about to attack me again. I glance back and see it's the New Yorker back for more.

He's a slow learner.

He bends down and reaches for my shirt again, but from my left side this time. I guess he doesn't think I have two hands.

I come up off my knees and paste him in the face with a stiff right cross. His knees buckle and he goes rolling back down the dock towards the house.

I turn my head slightly to watch him fall and see more trouble coming at me.

The woman who has beaten me bloody with the fly rod is headed my way dragging something heavy behind her.

Through the frothing lake water and blood, I have to blink hard twice to make out what she's doing.

She's carrying a pickaxe—the kind with a sharp point on one end and an adze face on the other end. The look on her face says she is looking forward to using the axe on me. She's 10 feet away.

I have my hands locked on the bruiser's forearms. I can feel him tiring. He's grunting now with the struggle. I only need a couple seconds more. I know I am that close to locking the second cuff on him. Greg and I will then be safe.

I decide to ignore the woman. I lean way out over the water as far as I can. "I got it, Greg!" I shout and I lock the second cuff around the man's wrist.

I'm so pleased with having handcuffed the guy, I forget the wild woman behind me.

Greg's eyes get huge and he looks up at me and screams, "Watch out!"

I duck. My lips kiss the dock and I swing both my arms up over my head as hard and fast as I can. There isn't time to pray.

I feel something like a baseball bat slam into my right bicep—where my head had been a second ago.

My arm feels like it's broken. I open my eyes and I see Greg's face. He looks like he's a witness to a train wreck.

I know I'm still alive.

I hear a KERPLOOSH off the dock—the sound a big rock makes when someone tosses it into the water.

She lost her grip when I blocked her swing. The axe has gone end over end into Big Lake.

I realize I was a second away from having my brains bashed in. Blood is streaming down my face from the head wounds she inflicted earlier.

Greg's face is bruised and swollen. One of his eyes is swelling shut.

We are both thinking the same thing, "These people are nuts! What in the world is wrong with them?"

The New Yorker says to the woman who just tried to take my head off, "I'm going up and get the rifle." He says it like he's going to get coffee.

These people want to kill us over nothing? This is insane!

If you haven't had the pleasure, I am here to tell you, adrenalin is a wonderful gift of Nature.

I relied on it often during my career. This was one of them.

I leap to my feet, grab the linebacker by the handcuff chain, yank hard and pull him up onto the dock, then drag him towards our boat.

He has nearly 80 pounds on me and is soaking wet besides.

Not a problem. I'm like a hungry jaguar who has latched onto an antelope twice her size and leaps into a tree for some fine dining.

No way am I going to let this guy get away.

Greg pulls himself up onto the dock behind me. He grabs the fellow's belt to help him move faster. I look up and see someone has untied our boat from the dock. It's drifted out about four feet.

"Grab his feet," I say to Greg. He nods and bends low.

"Ready?" We do a one, two, three sideways seesaw with the big man's body and then we toss the troublemaker into the boat.

I jump into the bow, force the prisoner to sit up and keep an eye on him. Greg jumps into the stern. The woman is screaming at us, trying to stop us from leaving, but she's temporarily out of artillery.

Greg yanks on the starter rope. The boat engine pops to life. He points the bow towards the center of the lake and gives it full throttle.

I look back and see someone running towards the end of the dock with a rifle.

I can't hear a thing over the roar of the boat motor. I hope they will think twice about pulling the trigger, knowing they might kill their friend instead of us.

When we get the big man to shore, I loosen the cuffs on his wrists and Greg and I take him straight to jail. But we're not there long.

All three of us end up at the hospital—the battler, Greg and me.

I had a broken nose and needed more than a dozen stitches in my head. Greg wasn't much better. The fellow that attacked us claimed he suffered a back injury when we tossed him in the boat.

We charged him and the woman who tried to kill me—with assault on a police officer. They countered with a lawsuit against the state of Maine.

Greg and I stumbled into a hornet's nest that day. Native American activists from Maine to Alaska were refusing to buy fishing and hunting licenses to bring attention to their multiple issues with the state and federal government.

Of course, we had no idea when we pulled up to the dock whether the fellow fishing was a native American or a Martian.

He was just a guy fishing. Maine law said he needed to have a fishing license and show it to us.

It would have been wrong for us to not ask to see the New Yorker's fishing license—to treat him differently than anybody else.

So how did this case end up? Well, my recollection is Maine paid the fellow we arrested a few thousand dollars to settle his claim.

The woman who beat me bloody with the fly reel and swung the pointy end of the pickaxe at my head, was fined $50 for simple assault.

The judge then suspended her sentence. She never paid a penny.

Law enforcement officers statewide were relieved when the tribes in Maine got their own lands and things quieted down.

A decade later, I was appointed Training Coordinator for the Warden Service Academy in Waterville.

The tribes sent their people to me for training, so they could enforce their laws on their own lands.

I made certain their candidates were treated the same as everyone else at the Academy.

I taught them to do the same when dealing with the public.

The tribes sent us good people, many of whom I would have been proud to hire as Maine wardens.

Kinda ironic, don't you think?

"He powers up the creaky crane and throws a lever forward, dropping the cherry picker jaws straight down through the metal roof of his garage."

Raccoon Revenge

I was working alongside Warden Lowell
Thomas in Waldo County for a few days. We
had stopped to fuel up and grab a quick
coffee, when a nervous fellow stepped out of an
old pick up truck and indicated he wanted to
have a chat.

The guy was maybe in his late 70s, his back
stooped like he was poised to pick a penny out of
the dirt at any time. He wore a heavy shirt with
frayed cuffs and the elbows worn out, showing a
plaid flannel shirt beneath.

His trousers were a couple sizes too big for him,
stained with grease and motor oil. He had blue
watery eyes and was missing a few teeth. A tired
John Deere cap was pulled tight to his ears.

When Lowell came out of the store with his
coffee, the man signaled my partner by tilting
his chin up sharply and raising the index finger
on his right hand two inches at the same time
—like a shy bidder at an auction.

I hung back inside the store and pretended to be

very interested in counting my change and made small talk with the sales clerk, to give them a few minutes alone.

Some guys won't talk if another warden they don't know is around.

Out of the corner of my eye, I see the man lean in and whisper something to Lowell, who has to bend his head down to listen.

After a few seconds, the fellow's head bounces up and down like a crow feasting on fresh road kill in the middle of a busy highway.

A smart crow stays vigilant knowing an oncoming vehicle could flatten him fast too. This fellow was looking up and down the road the same way. It was clear he didn't want folks seeing him talking to a warden.

But the parking lot was empty except for the store clerk's car, our cruiser and his old Chevy. He was willing to take a chance.

I see a new issue of Uncle Henry's in the news stand and am just reaching for it when Lowell shoots me a glance.

I know that's my signal to join him.

I smile at the sales clerk, drop my change in my pocket and step outside.

Lowell introduces me to Edwin. The fellow nods,
skips the small talk and asks, "You know that
logger feller up on Hancock Road?"

Lowell nods and says, "You mean André?
A big guy who lives up off that tight corner, with
his house set back off the road 50 yards or so?
Kinda has a junkyard around his place?"

The man looks right, then left and spits a wad of
chewing tobacco juice into the dirt.

He leans in closer and says with disgust, "Yeah.
That's him. That's the feller I'm talking about
—big mouth with a gray beard. I believe you
fellows have caught him several times before."

Lowell gives a short nod in the affirmative.
I know the guy too. Lowell and I have both cited
André before.

"Well, what's up?" Lowell asks.

"I hear he's training dogs to hunt raccoons, and
to make it easy, he's gone and trapped some
young 'coons and is keepin' them penned up at
his place."

He pauses, takes a step back and spits out more
brown juice. Then he comes back in towards us
and shakes his head.

"I just don't think that's right to use them babies

like 'at. I've hunted 'coons plenty, but that ain't right," he says and spits again for emphasis.

Then he leans in so he's about nose to chin with Lowell and his eyes get big like he is telling us where to find a treasure map.

"It ain't legal neither, 'tis it?" he asks and he looks intently at both our faces with pleading, bloodshot eyes.

It was clear he wanted Lowell or me to say, "No Sir, it sure ain't!" and to get all riled up, hitch up our pants, jump on our horses and go galloping towards André's place with guns a'blazin'—like we were lawmen in an old Hollywood movie.

The glint in Edwin's eyes implied he had a big problem with André and he was counting on us to pay him back for the slight. That's the way it often works with outlaws. Once they have a falling out, all bets are off. It's not unusual for both sides to start telling stories to a lawman.

Lowell purses his lips and nods and tells Edwin, "No, you can't keep any wildlife caged." Then he looks over at me.

When André wasn't pulling a fast one on someone, he worked as a logger and backyard mechanic and occasionally raised beef, pigs and chickens.

He was the kind of guy who had the brains
to be a success, but instead of playing by the
rules, he spent all his time scheming to take
advantage of the next person to come his way.

His wife and kids had left him years ago.

Now close to 50 years old, all he had left were
his big ideas, some tired machinery and a mean
streak that just wouldn't quit.

Lowell's informant opens his mouth to tell us
something else, when he spies a rusty sedan
rattling down the road, signaling to turn into
the parking lot.

His mouth slams shut like a bass on a peeper
popper. He dips his head low, spits, turns and
scuttles over to his pick up truck like a crab
running from a seagull.

There wasn't so much as a nod of goodbye.

"You know that guy well?" I ask Lowell, as
Edwin rolls out of the parking lot and heads up
the road.

"Edwin's given me several tips over the years,"
Lowell says. "There's probably some truth in
what he's saying."

Lowell and I walk to the cruiser, sit and sip our
coffee and discuss this tip.

We've got a couple problems here. First and foremost, this informant hadn't given us a clue as to where the raccoons were being kept. André owned a good bit of land, along with his home and outbuildings.

He wouldn't be likely to have the animals caged in his yard for anyone to see when they pulled in. He would have them hidden. But where?

André was also famous for a short fuse, which he used to intimidate and threaten people. He liked nothing more than getting nose to nose with a guy and screaming his lungs out like some made for TV wrestler in the ring.

His reputation as a hothead worked well for him. If a guy to whom he owed money or work asked André to pay up, André would slam his big fist down on a bar top or truck hood and start yelling at the guy, telling him he didn't know what he was talking about.

Most guys would just give up and walk away rather than fight.

André reacted to any inquiry from a law enforcement officer in the same way. Lowell and I could be certain there would be drama when we caught up with André to inquire about this allegation.

Well, there was only one way to get answers, so

Lowell turned the key in the ignition and we headed on over to André's.

It was around 10 a.m. when we arrived.

We were greeted by four hound dogs and a Beagle. They were chained to crudely constructed doghouses with tarpaper roofs, grouped together in the shade of a big willow tree.

The dogs wriggled and barked when we pulled in, but quieted down quickly when we ignored them.

We waited for André to walk out of the house. Despite a half dozen trucks and cars in the yard, it didn't appear he was home.

But the presence of the hounds gave some credence to the tipster's tale. André wasn't the type to have dogs around just because he enjoyed their company. He had to believe they would make him money.

Lowell and I stepped out of the cruiser and started looking around. If André had the raccoons hidden outside somewhere there would be a trail leading to a pen.

We walked over to a 28 x 80 foot sheet metal shop André used for storage and machinery repairs. The big overhead door was pulled shut.

There were four wooden, double hung windows on each side of the garage to let in a little daylight.

Clumps of Box Elder trees, brush and burdocks were growing alongside the shop's foundation. Lowell suggested we traipse through the tangle, and try to peer inside the windows.

"The raccoons might be in there," he suggested.

"That's a good idea," I said. "I'll meet you back out front in a few minutes. If you see anything, holler."

I get to the first window and squint. The pane is so dirty and the interior so dark, I can only make out shadowy truck and car parts piled high.

I push on and am just about to stare through the third window when Lowell calls out to me.

I see he's shining his flashlight through the window on his side. The light cuts a path across the garage floor.

"Parker! Do you see them? Look off to your left," Lowell shouts to me.

I cup my hands over my eyes to block the sun's glare behind me and press my nose tighter against the grimy pane.

I see something—like a fuzzy cat—race across
the cement.

Lowell bangs his fist twice on the side of the
metal building, startling me.

I'm not the only one he's surprised. With
his beam illuminating the concrete floor, I
see four young raccoons skedaddle over and
around a maze of engine blocks, tire piles,
buckets of hydraulic fluid, mound of mufflers
and rusted tail pipes. Their eyes glow green
when Lowell's light shines directly on their
faces.

"Yup, I see them," I grin and yell back to Lowell.
"I'll meet you back out front."

Two minutes later, as Lowell and I stand outside
the cruiser discussing our next move while
pulling green burdocks off our trousers, we
hear a truck engine climbing up the driveway
towards us.

Its André and when he sees the cruiser and two
wardens in his yard waiting for him, he gets a
maniacal look on his face.

He punches the truck's gas pedal and aims
it at our car, then slams on the brakes just
six feet short of ramming our cruiser broadside.
A cloud of dust billows up from around his tires
and he grins with satisfaction.

He flings open his driver's door and before he's even set a foot on the truck's running board, he's screaming at us, "Get off my property! You got no right to be here!"

His eyes are bulging, his face is beet red and the cords in his neck tighten like someone is strangling him.

Spit flies—and since he's downwind of a slight breeze—the majority of his spittle settles into his bushy gray beard.

It makes André appear as if he's been exposed to rabies.

Lowell and I know better. This is just André's way of greeting law enforcement officers. We expected nothing less.

André jumps down from his truck and storms over to us with his fists balled up and his eyes popped like a Sea Robin yanked out of Casco Bay.

"What do you want?" he screams at us.

Lowell holds his ground and calmly tells André, "We have information you have live raccoons caged. That's against the law. You can't have wild animals in captivity. They have to be free to come and go."

André gets in Lowell's face, barely two feet away,

shouting and flailing his arms like a threatened rooster.

Lowell doesn't budge.

"We're here on official business. And your land is not posted against trespass," he tells André, without raising his voice. "Now, step back!"

I don't speak. I'm four feet from Lowell's side, poised to leap if André is crazy enough to take a swing at my partner.

"Raccoons?" André shouts like we're insane.

He makes a face like he just took a swig of spoiled milk and says again, "Raccoons?" as if he doesn't know what we are talking about. I notice he's not answering Lowell's question.

Lowell sighs.

"Warden Tripp and I took a little stroll around your garage before you showed up," Lowell says, with a nod towards the shop.

He is giving André an opportunity to confess.

André stops sputtering, plants his feet and glowers at Lowell like a fox about to have a rabbit snatched from his jaws.

He doesn't speak.

"We both saw the raccoons inside. You have to let them out. They have to be free. That's the law," Lowell says.

André knows we got him.

He stumbles back a few paces at the news from Lowell, like he's just been punched hard in the gut or just got some real bad news from the bank.

If he was angry before, he's apoplectic now, knowing we looked through the shop windows before he arrived.

André turns away from us.

His eyes are searching for something around the yard. It's like he's lost interest in this conversation and is looking for a wrench.

He's up to something.

We're surrounded by a sea of junk. He has at least 50 choices of deadly iron within 20 feet of where we are standing. From axles to disc brakes to tie rods, it's all here.

I'm thinking maybe he's considering grabbing a length of steel pipe and swinging it at our heads.

His eyes settle on his pulp log truck.

He glares back at us and grins, runs over to his rig, jumps in the cab and fires it up.

Clouds of black smoke spew from the stack.

Lloyd and I look at each other with raised eyebrows. We don't speak. We stand there wondering what could possibly be next.

André throws the truck into second gear and steers it towards the garage. The engine is cold and tired. The truck lurches and bucks as he urges it on. I see him screaming at the machine from behind the dash.

He gets within 12 feet of the garage, throws the truck into neutral and sets the parking brake.

The cab door flies open with a big squawk like it is begging for hinge grease. André jumps out of the driver's seat, climbs up the ladder to the loader like an angry orangutan, plops his large behind into the torn seat and grabs the controls with his meaty paws.

The boom comes to life. It squeaks and groans in protest. The truck stack belches more black smoke.

André is shouting words we can't make out, glaring at us and grinning.

The claws rise out of their cradle, he swings the

arm above his shop roof and then raises the boom as high as it will go.

He sees us struggling to hear his words.

He stops and quiets the engine just long enough for us to hear him shout, "Raccoons? You're worried about raccoons??? I'll give you 'coons!"

He powers up the creaky crane and throws a lever forward, dropping the cherry picker jaws straight down through the metal roof of his garage.

Trusses creak and crack, screws pop, the metal roofing buckles and rips.

Lowell and I stand in awe as André lifts the boom and swings the jaws back and forth inside his shop. He has to push the torn metal edges and widen the hole to lift the jaws out.

He lifts the claws high up in the air again, turns the boom five feet to the right and releases them again, slamming through a new section, just beside the first hole.

He grimaces and throws the handles forward and back, forward and back, like he's ratcheting tight a heavy log load. The hydraulic hoses bounce, his truck wobbles and the metal roof screams.

He shakes and shimmies until the two roof
holes become one.

Lowell and I are highly trained professionals,
schooled in the art of hiding our emotions.
But watching a man destroy his garage?

This is a first.

I can't hide my astonishment.

André sees the look on my face.

He throws his head back like he's the Phantom
of the Opera and lost in the music. I can't hear
him, but it looks like he is laughing.

He moves the boom another 10 feet down the
roof and slams a third hole into the garage—just
for good measure, I guess.

When he's satisfied with his handiwork, he
lifts the boom high, swings the jaws away from
what's left of his garage roof and lowers them
artfully into the cradle.

Then, with a flourish befitting a musician, he
releases the levers like he's just finished an
inspired keyboard solo.

He lifts his arms high and bows his head.
He's savoring the moment, like he's hearing the
applause from a sold out crowd at Carnegie Hall.

When he lifts his head, he sneers at Lowell and me.

Then, he climbs down from the seat, steps onto the running board of the truck, reaches for the ignition key and shuts the diesel engine down.

With silence settling in around us, André drops to the ground and laughs like a madman. He's relishing his "I showed you!" moment.

I don't let on, but I am impressed. I have never witnessed this level of insanity before.

I look up at the roof. He's dug a hole big enough to drive a bus through.

I'd heard rumors André had burned his house down for the insurance money a few years earlier. I'm thinking this time, maybe he'll tell the insurance company his shop was hit by a meteor.

But I'm having trouble connecting the dots in André's thinking. He's like a driver who gets pulled over for speeding by a state trooper and the guy gets so upset he torches his car thinking he's getting rid of the evidence.

I can't wait to see what he does for an encore.

André pulls up his pants and with a victor's swagger he takes a few steps towards us, points up to the roof and shouts out, "There!"

He has a big smile of satisfaction on his face. "The raccoons are free to go," he declares. "I hope you're happy."

Lowell and I stare up at the roof. For the first time in 20 minutes, there's no shouting, no engines roaring.

That's when we hear it—the sound of fingernails scratching metal—coming from inside the garage, and boards tumbling.

It's the raccoons. They are, in fact, making the most of this blue sky opportunity their captor has given them.

They are making a dash for freedom.

Lowell and I step back another 20 feet so we can get a better look at the roof holes. Here come the raccoons. They pull their way up the shattered trusses and clamber through the holes.

They run for the branches of the Box Elders on the far side of the shop and disappear into the greenery in a matter of seconds.

André points to them, smiles and says to Lowell, "See! They're free. I've done what you wanted. So, we're all good, all done. Now, get off my property," and he turns his back to us and starts walking towards his house.

259

But Lowell isn't satisfied.

"No, we're not done," he tells André. "Warden Tripp and I are going inside your shop to make certain all the raccoons are out of there."

André stops in his tracks, spins around and clenches his fists.

"You got no right to be going in my garage!" he says, running at Lowell and raising his voice to a beller again. "I let 'em go. You just seen 'em go! I've done what you wanted."

"Now, I want you outta here," André adds, pointing at his driveway.

Lowell ignores André. He walks past him towards a side door on the shop, turns the handle and steps inside.

I hang back a little to make certain André doesn't attack Lowell from behind.

Once inside the building, Lowell pulls the chain that opens the big overhead door. Daylight floods the garage.

I stroll past André to help Lowell look around.

Lowell turns on his flashlight and methodically inspects the interior—listening and looking for any sign of caged raccoons.

He walks to the back of the shop, shines his light along the back wall, then turns and heads back slowly towards me.

And that's when Lowell finds it—behind an old truck frame and a stack of tractor tires —a freshly killed spike horn.

It was hanging by a chain stout enough to support a musk ox. The hide was still on the little buck.

I see Lowell stop and smile. He calls out, "Parker, over here!" Lowell figures André had shot it the night before, just a few hours before our arrival.

Now we know why André had entertained us with an Academy Award winning performance of a logger gone loco.

André knew if we found that deer he was facing some serious jail time. This wasn't going to be his first citation for poaching—or his second or even his third.

And that's why André was willing to literally blow the roof off his shop to make us go away. He needed to keep us from finding the bigger prize—that little jacked deer.

As a habitual offender, the buck gave Lowell a reason to handcuff André on the spot and give

him a ride to jail. Now, in addition to a charge
of illegally keeping wildlife, we had him for
poaching too.

Oh sure, we had to listen to André cuss, moan,
screech and kick the back of our seat like a four
year old all the way to Waterville.

But it was like music to our ears. More
entertainment. We left him in a cell, went to a
diner to have lunch and celebrate. We couldn't
stop laughing.

Lowell and I compared notes on guys who had
tried to hide fish or game from us over the years.
Some were pretty ingenious.

But we agreed André had set the bar so high
this day it was hard to imagine anyone ever
topping his demented tour de force.

A few weeks later, André went before a judge
who was tired of seeing him in his courtroom.
André was handed a $3,000 fine and spent 10
days in jail. He also lost his right to hunt and
fish for five years.

That meant André wouldn't need his hounds
anytime soon. In dog years, they'd qualify for
Medicare before André could purchase another
hunting license.

They all got new homes.

As for André's new shop skylight, well, that wasn't going to be an easy or inexpensive fix.

Someone would have to pull a big section of the roof off, replace the crushed trusses and then install a new metal roof. That meant more money out of André's wallet.

Whether Lowell's informant, Edwin, really cared about those little raccoons or he just wanted to pay André back for some deal gone bad, I never found out.

But Edwin—and the raccoons—sure had their revenge.

Acknowledgements

*This book could not have been completed
without the encouragement and skill
of the following individuals:*

**Jean McHenry, Inge Schaefer,
Dorrice and John Hammer,
Carrie Cook, Bob Lutz,
Sandy Brisson, Jean Cross,
Al and Karen Myers,
W. Douglas Darby, Paul A. Young,
Robert Rooks, Sam Stanley,
Eric and Ingrid Nuse,
Patsy Munson, Tamara Walker,
and O.C.**

Thank you, one and all!

265

PARKER WITH BLACK
BEAR CUB, WOOFER.

PARKER IN SMELT
FISHING DISGUISE.

CHIEF WARDEN PARKER TRIPP

WHO WE ARE

 **Megan Price** is a former award winning journalist and magazine writer. She enjoys turning good stories into great books.

 **Bob Lutz** is a talented caricaturist, creating quirky illustrations. Bob is also a retired Vermont Fish & Game Warden.

 **Carrie Cook** is an exceptional graphic designer and upright bass player who lives in Cambridge, Vermont.

Want more great warden stories?

Volume 1

Volume 2

Volume 3

Visit www.VermontWild.com